REGENTS RESTORATION DRAMA SERIES

General Editor: John Loftis

P9-DEF-696

THE GRUB-STREET OPERA

HENRY FIELDING

The Grub-Street Opera

Edited by

EDGAR V. ROBERTS

UNIVERSITY OF NEBRASKA PRESS · LINCOLN

MANUFACTURED IN THE UNITED STATES OF AMERICA

Regents Restoration Drama Series

The Regents Restoration Drama Series provides soundly edited texts, in modern spelling, of the more significant plays of the late seventeenth and early eighteenth centuries. The word "Restoration" is here used ambiguously and must be explained. If to the historian it refers to the period between 1660 and 1685 (or 1688), it has long been used by the student of drama in default of a more precise word to refer to plays belonging to the dramatic tradition established in the 1660's, weakening after 1700, and displaced in the 1730's. It is in this extended sense—imprecise though justified by academic custom— that the word is used in this series, which includes plays first produced between 1660 and 1737. Although these limiting dates are determined by political events, the return of Charles II (and the removal of prohibitions against operation of theaters) and the passage of Walpole's Stage Licensing Act, they enclose a period of dramatic history having a coherence of its own in the establishment, development, and disintegration of a tradition.

Some fifteen editions having appeared as this volume goes to press, the series has reached perhaps a third of its anticipated range of between forty and fifty volumes. The volumes will continue to be published for a number of years, at the rate of three or more annually. From the beginning the editors have planned the series with attention to the projected dimensions of the completed whole, a representative collection of Restoration drama providing a record of artistic achievement and providing also a record of the deepest concerns of three generations of Englishmen. And thus it contains deservedly famous plays—*The Country Wife*, *The Man of Mode*, and *The Way of the World*— and also significant but little known plays, *The Virtuoso*, for example, and *City Politiques*, the former a satirical review of scientific investigation in the early years of the Royal Society, the latter an equally satirical review of politics at the time of the Popish Plot. If the volumes of famous plays finally achieve the larger circulation, the other volumes may conceivably have the greater utility, in making available texts otherwise difficult of access with the editorial apparatus needed to make them intelligible.

The editors have had the instructive example of the parallel and senior project, the Regents Renaissance Drama Series; they have in fact used the editorial policies developed for the earlier plays as their own, modifying them as appropriate for the later period and as the experience of successive editions suggested. The introductions to the separate Restoration plays differ considerably in their nature. Although a uniform body of relevant information is presented in each of them, no attempt has been made to impose a pattern of interpretation. Emphasis in the introductions has necessarily varied with the nature of the plays and inevitably—we think desirably— with the special interests and aptitudes of the different editors.

Each text in the series is based on a fresh collation of the seventeenth- and eighteenth-century editions that might be presumed to have authority. The textual notes, which appear above the rule at the bottom of each page, record all substantive departures from the edition used as the copy-text. Variant substantive readings among contemporary editions are listed there as well. Editions later than the eighteenth century are referred to in the textual notes only when an emendation originating in some one of them is received into the text· Variants of accidentals (spelling, punctuation, capitalization) are not recorded in the notes. Contracted forms of characters' names are silently expanded in speech prefixes and stage directions, and, in the case of speech prefixes, are regularized. Additions to the stage directions of the copy-text are enclosed in brackets.

Spelling has been modernized along consciously conservative lines, but within the limits of a modernized text the linguistic quality of the original has been carefully preserved. Contracted preterites have regularly been expanded. Punctuation has been brought into accord with modern practice. The objective has been to achieve a balance between the pointing of the old editions and a system of punctuation which, without overloading the text with exclamation marks, semicolons, and dashes, will make the often loosely flowing verse and prose of the original syntactically intelligible to the modern reader. Dashes are regularly used only to indicate interrupted speeches, or shifts of address within a single speech.

Explanatory notes, chiefly concerned with glossing obsolete words and phrases, are printed below the textual notes at the bottom of each page. References to stage directions in the notes follow the admirable system of the Revels editions, whereby stage directions are keyed, decimally, to the line of the text before or after which they occur.

Thus, a note on 0.2 has reference to the second line of the stage direction at the beginning of the scene in question. A note on 115.1 has reference to the first line of the stage direction following line 115 of the text of the relevant scene. Speech prefixes, and any stage directions attached to them, are keyed to the first line of accompanying dialogue.

JOHN LOFTIS

October, 1967
Stanford University

Contents

List of Abbreviations

Bailey   Nathaniel Bailey. *An Universal Etymological English Dictionary*. London, 1733.

Cross   Wilbur L. Cross. *The History of Henry Fielding*. 3 vols. New Haven, 1918.

Egmont   *The Dairy of the Earl of Egmont*. Historical Manuscripts Commission. London, 1920–1923.

GGSO   *The Genuine Grub-Street Opera*. London, 1731.

GSO   *The Grub-Street Opera*. London. (The title page bears the date 1731.)

Lucas   Reginald Lucas. *George II and His Ministers*. London, 1910.

OED   *Oxford English Dictionary*

S.D.   stage direction

WO   *The Welsh Opera*. London, 1731.

Introduction

The version of *The Grub-Street Opera* customarily printed in Fielding's works, and the basis of the present edition, bears on its title page the imprint of James Roberts and the date 1731.[1] The copy-text is in the British Museum (press mark 643. h. 19). A collation with copies in the Bodleian, Folger, and Huntington libraries indicates that there are no substantive variants. Occasionally I have accepted readings from the earlier versions of the play (*The Welsh Opera* and *The Genuine Grub-Street Opera*), and I have supplied stage directions, liberally, when the sense of the play requires them; when there are clear errors in the copy-text I have corrected them. All changes are recorded in the textual notes.

The two earlier versions of *The Grub-Street Opera* were both printed in 1731. The first of these, *The Welsh Opera*, is the only one to have been performed before an eighteenth-century audience. Apparently the text represents the version of the play as it was produced at the New Theatre in the Haymarket in the spring of 1731. *The Welsh Opera* was published on June 26, 1731, by E. Rayner, who was

[1] Despite the title-page date, there is no other evidence that *The Grub-Street Opera*, as distinguished from *The Welsh Opera* and *The Genuine Grub-Street Opera*, was published in 1731. Usually, when a play was published in this period, it was advertised in one of the daily or weekly papers. There are no advertisements for *The Grub-Street Opera*, even though the two earlier, spurious versions of the play were advertised. The first advertisement for the play, in fact, was not printed until 1765, and the first reliable date for the existence of the play is 1755, when it was included in the second volume of a collected set of Fielding's plays published by Andrew Millar, who had acquired the rights to all the plays at about this time. Moreover, the relatively modern typographical appearance of *The Grub-Street Opera* supports a date of publication far later than 1731. For these and a number of other reasons, I believe that the play was published perhaps in the 1740's and possibly just at the time in the mid-1750's when Millar was gathering the plays for his edition of Fielding's complete dramatic works. But the whole matter of the date of *The Grub-Street Opera* is too problematical and detailed for further discussion here. If one chooses to accept the title-page date, he must concede that the publication was singularly unheralded.

sympathetic to the political opponents of Sir Robert Walpole. It seems clear that Fielding did not authorize this publication and had nothing to do with its printing; indeed, some scholars have assumed that he was the author of an anonymous notice in *The Daily Post* of June 28 which claimed that *The Welsh Opera* was "incorrect and spurious" and that Rayner was a "notorious Paper Pyrate." The next version of the play, *The Genuine Grub-Street Opera*, was published on August 18, 1731, for the benefit of the actors of the New Theatre in the Haymarket. Though this edition lacks two scenes, it is presumably the text of the play as Fielding revised it and presented it to the actors of the New Theatre for rehearsal. This version was never, to my knowledge, performed, and like *The Welsh Opera* it was published without Fielding's authorization. Thus, *The Grub-Street Opera* is the only reliable basis for a modern text.

The Grub-Street Opera is the most audacious, ambitious, and tuneful of Fielding's nine extant ballad operas. It is more like the prototype of all ballad operas, *The Beggar's Opera*, than any of his other plays. It contains sixty-five songs, only four fewer than *The Beggar's Opera*, and eight of its ballad tunes had been popularized in Gay's play. In a few of its scenes and songs it echoes *The Beggar's Opera*, and like its model it is divided into three acts (the characteristic of an "irregular" as opposed to "regular" five-act drama). In the mode of Gay's political burlesque, *The Grub-Street Opera* is an allegory of political England in 1731, with characters who represent important political figures, including Sir Robert Walpole and even King George II, Queen Caroline, and their oldest son Frederick Louis, Prince of Wales. Walpole is ridiculed throughout the play, and Caroline and Frederick are treated with especial severity.

The political nature of *The Grub-Street Opera* created problems for Fielding, but it also presented him with a great opportunity. When he began his career as a dramatist, he attempted to have his plays produced at the Theatre-Royal in Drury Lane, one of the two patent theaters in London. Though he was successful with his first play, *Love in Several Masques* (1728), he was not with his second, and turned in 1730 to the New Theatre in the Haymarket, which operated without a patent. Since the actors there were not highly skilled and the audiences there liked satire, he turned his talents away from serious five-act drama to farce and burlesque, with a pronouncedly satiric bent.

His first play for the New Haymarket was *The Author's Farce* (1730), a ballad opera which satirized the London literary and social scene from the point of view of the principal character, a young dramatist like Fielding himself.[2] As this immediately successful play showed, Fielding was a master of irregular, topical drama, and, on the strength of similar plays, in the following year he became the major playwright for the theater. In April, 1730, he produced and published the popular *Tom Thumb*, and in June, 1730, he saw into production the less successful *Rape Upon Rape*, a five-act farce. He reworked *Rape Upon Rape* into *The Coffee-House Politician* by November, 1730, and at this time he presumably began his revision of *Tom Thumb*, and wrote an afterpiece entitled *The Letter Writers*. This double bill, with *Tom Thumb* renamed *The Tragedy of Tragedies; or, The Life and Death of Tom Thumb the Great*, was produced on March 24, 1731.[3] Thus, during the year following *The Author's Farce*, audiences at the New Theatre in the Haymarket were presented with four plays by Fielding, all satirical.

The Letter Writers was not well received; when it was withdrawn after the third night (March 29) Fielding found himself in need of a new afterpiece for the popular *Tragedy of Tragedies*. His effort, the first version of *The Grub-Street Opera*, was *The Welsh Opera*, and it came speedily from his pen. An advertisement in *The Daily Post* of April 6, 1731, indicates that the play was already in rehearsal, for the advertisement stated that the play would be "deferr'd till Easter week" (i.e., the week following April 18). Following this date the theater presented *The Author's Farce* (probably merely the third-act puppet show entitled *The Pleasure of the Town*) four times as an afterpiece for *The Tragedy of Tragedies*. Finally, on April 17 it was announced that the new farce would accompany the performance of *The Tragedy of Tragedies* on Wednesday, April 21. For some reason, however, there

[2] See Charles B. Woods, ed., *The Author's Farce* (Lincoln, Nebr., 1966).

[3] All dates in this introduction may be verified in Arthur H. Scouten, ed., *The London Stage, 1660–1800; Part 3: 1729–1747* (Carbondale, Ill., 1961), Vol. I; and Allardyce Nicoll, *A History of English Drama, 1660–1900; Volume II: Early Eighteenth Century Drama*, 3rd ed. (Cambridge, 1952). For discussions of *The Grub-Street Opera* see Wilbur L. Cross, *The History of Henry Fielding* (New Haven, 1918), I, 103 ff.; F. Homes Dudden, *Henry Fielding, His Life, Works, and Times* (Oxford, 1952), I, 75 ff.; Jack Richard Brown, "Henry Fielding's *Grub-Street Opera*," *Modern Language Quarterly*, XVI (1955), 32–41; and John Loftis, *The Politics of Drama in Augustan England* (Oxford, 1963), p. 105.

was a further delay of one day, and *The Welsh Opera* received its première on April 22. Although Wilbur L. Cross suggests that the management deferred the play because of its political satire,[4] I think it more likely that the delay resulted from the difficulty of rehearsing and producing the play in so short a time. With the already established *Tragedy of Tragedies*, *The Welsh Opera* was immediately popular. It was performed again on Friday and the following Monday, and for the fourth performance, Fielding's benefit night, tickets were in such demand that the theater management raised the cost of pit tickets from the customary three shillings to five (*Daily Post*, April 28).

It was obviously this success that caused Fielding to turn his short play into a main piece of three acts, for such an enthusiastic response gave promise that an expansion would bring more profitable benefit nights. We may surmise that he worked busily on his revision during May, 1731, while the New Haymarket company, in addition to its benefits, performed an anonymous allegorical attack on Sir Robert Walpole called *The Fall of Mortimer*.[5] As Fielding was expanding his play into *The Grub-Street Opera*, he also made "several Alterations and Additions" to *The Welsh Opera*. This altered version was produced six times, the first time on May 19. A playhouse copy of this altered version might have been the basis of E. Rayner's edition of *The Welsh Opera* published on June 26.

By May 31, 1731, Fielding had completed *The Grub-Street Opera* and turned it over to the actors at the New Theatre in the Haymarket. Apparently they first decided to postpone the play until autumn; however, according to *The Daily Post* of May 31, certain unspecified "Persons of Quality" urged immediate production and galvanized the company into rehearsal, with plans to produce the play "within a Fortnight." If this report was indeed true, and not merely a puff preliminary, it would appear that the "Persons of Quality" were sympathetic to the Opposition (that is, the Tories and disaffected Whigs who united to oppose Walpole and his policies), if not important figures in it.

Plans were also apparently made to publish the text of the play in time for the "first Night of Performance," according to *The Daily Post* of May 31. This report is tantalizing and puzzling, for it indicates a publication of *The Grub-Street Opera* that has not yet been discovered

---

[4] Cross, I, 107.

[5] See Cross, I, 107 f., and Loftis, pp. 105 f., for discussions of this play.

by any major library or book collector. As described in the report, the edition was to contain about sixty songs with the music "prefix'd" to each song. This method of printing music was common in the ballad operas published by John Watts, who printed the music of each song immediately above the words, setting the text as a lyric poem. Such an arrangement, however, is not employed in any available copies of *The Grub-Street Opera*. In fact, no known text of the play prior to the present edition has ever included music. If the newspaper report was accurate—and it may not have been—either the edition was totally withdrawn before the expected date of publication, or else it was published but has been lost. The first alternative seems the more likely.

Once *The Grub-Street Opera* went into rehearsal, *The Welsh Opera* was abandoned (*Daily Post*, June 5), its stage history complete after ten performances. In order to get the new play ready for the well-publicized première on June 11, the "exceeding busy" actors of the New Haymarket gave no performances of any play after Monday, June 7 (*Daily Post*, June 9). *The Grub-Street Opera* was not performed on June 11, however; *The Daily Post* of June 12 reported that "The Principal Performer" [i.e., William Mullart] had "been taken violently ill." The first performance was then advertised for the following Monday (June 14), but on that date it was replaced by *The Fall of Mortimer* together with *The Jealous Taylor*, an anonymous and apparently unpublished ballad opera. In the advertisement for these two plays, the management of the New Theatre in the Haymarket noted that "we are obliged to defer the GRUBSTREET OPERA till further Notice." There is no evidence that the notice ever came, or that Fielding's ambitious revision was ever performed.

One is unquestionably justified in doubting the explanation for the deferment, and in supposing that the snuffing-out of both the performance and publication of *The Grub-Street Opera* indicates strong political activities behind the scenes. Most probably, these activities were originated by someone in the Government, for the year 1731 had become politically stormy. The Opposition had been carrying on a war against the Ministry along many fronts, of which the stage of the New Theatre in the Haymarket was only one. In January the high political animosity reached the point of violence when a duel (burlesqued by Fielding in II.iii) was fought by William Pulteney and John, Lord Hervey. Lord Hervey was wounded in the encounter. Aroused by this incident and by the subsequent attacks of Opposition writers, the Government retaliated by legal means in May, June, and July, 1731: Richard Francklin, who published the Opposition weekly, *The Country Journal, or The Craftsman*, was arrested twice. Then, in July, two "private Sentinels" were "committed to the Savoy prison for singing a treasonable song at Windsor," and their court martial was scheduled for September (*Daily Journal*, Sept. 3). After *The Grub-Street Opera* was withdrawn, the New Theatre in the Haymarket experienced severe governmental repression. On July 5 a Grand Jury delivered a presentment against *The Fall of Mortimer*, along with some other works; when the New Haymarket actors tried to perform this play later in the month, a group of constables appeared, armed with a warrant from "several Justices of the Peace, to seize Mr. Mullet [sic], who play'd the Part of Mortimer, and the rest of the Performers" (*Daily Journal*, July 22). Though the actors "all made their Escapes," their theater was now under the threat of renewed governmental harassment.

Under this threat, there appears to have been dissension among the company. In August, a rehearsal copy of *The Grub-Street Opera* was published for the "Benefit of the Comedians" as the previously mentioned *Genuine Grub-Street Opera*. Some of the actors disavowed the edition in the daily papers, claiming that none of the company was responsible for the publication. Yet when, on August 19, the day after publication, the company attempted to perform *Hurlothrumbo* by Samuel Johnson of Cheshire, the constables stopped the performance and once again attempted to arrest the actors (who all escaped). Though some observers have claimed that Johnson's play could be presented as a political satire, there is no proof that the company had this intention; moreover, Walpole himself had subscribed to its first publication. It would therefore appear that the Government suppressed the performance not because of *Hurlothrumbo* itself but simply because in performing it the actors were showing their defiance. There is an additional possibility that the closing was intended as punishment for those actors who had arranged for the publication of *The Genuine Grub-Street Opera*. Whatever the reason, however, the continued threat of constabulary intervention effectively ended all performances at the New Theatre in the Haymarket for the indefinite future.

While the actors were experiencing these difficulties, Fielding was silent. His silence is enigmatic, for *The Grub-Street Opera*, if it was indeed suppressed by the Ministry, was potentially a *cause célèbre* for the Opposition. One might remember that Gay had acquired a small fortune in 1729 from the publication of his *Polly*, which had been stopped in rehearsal by the Lord Chamberlain.[6] Angered by the suppression, Gay's friends and sympathizers hastened to subscribe to the edition and to purchase copies of it. But while freedom of expression was as strong an issue in 1731 as in 1729, there is no record that Fielding raised it in order to promote his play, even though E. Rayner and the actors of the New Theatre in the Haymarket obviously capitalized upon it in their unauthorized editions. The abrupt and uncontested demise of *The Grub-Street Opera* leads one to conclude that Fielding saw his best interests in ending the play's life and in concealing or obscuring his reasons for doing so.

His activities during the remainder of 1731 are also obscure. At some time in this period, he arranged with the patentees of the Theatre-Royal in Drury Lane (where he had tried to produce plays in 1730) to have his plays performed there. He had completed the new affiliation by December, and in the four following years at Drury Lane he maintained his position as one of London's principal dramatists.

The troubled history of *The Grub-Street Opera* is a graphic reminder of the extent of Fielding's political satire. Although time has obscured the significance of the personalities and issues brought out in the play, the government of Sir Robert Walpole obviously thought that Fielding had gone to extremes. To show the nature of his political burlesque, I have prepared the following list, which indicates the person that each principal character in the drama was designed to portray:

Sir Owen Apshinken	George II
Master Owen Apshinken	Frederick Louis, Prince of Wales
Lady Apshinken	Queen Caroline
Parson Puzzletext	The exact person is not clear. Perhaps Puzzletext represents Dr. Samuel Clarke, who had served as Caroline's spiritual adviser until his death in 1729. Other possibilities are Bishop Hoadly, who was

6 William Henry Irving, *John Gay, Favorite of the Wits* (Durham, N.C., 1940), pp. 272 ff.

in particular favor with Caroline; Bishop Butler, Caroline's Clerk of the Closet, who discoursed frequently with her on religious subjects; and Francis Hare, Dean of St. Paul's, a controversialist also in Caroline's favor. Whether Puzzletext represents a person or not, however, he is clearly intended to mock Caroline's religious interests.

Robin   Sir Robert Walpole

John   John, Lord Hervey

Thomas   Thomas Pelham-Holles, Duke of Newcastle, Secretary of State for the Southern Department and later Prime Minister. Newcastle was a staunch Whig who threw his weight and fortune behind Walpole, and organized a vast machinery of political persuasion and bribery. Because Thomas is pictured as an opponent and not as a friend of Robin, Fielding's allegory is here inconsistent.[7]

Sweetissa   Maria or Molly Skerrit, Walpole's mistress

The only symbol of the Opposition is William, who stands for William Pulteney, the Opposition leader. There is no reason to assume that either Susan or Margery is an allegorical figure. The same is true of Mr. Apshones and Molly, although Molly may be intended as a general figure representing the many ladies pursued by Prince Frederick.[8] The name *Molly* also suggests Molly Skerrit.

[7] See Stebelton H. Nulle, "The Duke of Newcastle and the Election of 1727," *Journal of Modern History*, IX (1937), 1–22; and Basil Williams, "The Duke of Newcastle and the Elections of 1734," *English Historical Review*, XII (1897), 448–488.

[8] Before coming to England in 1728, the Prince of Wales had futilely courted Princess Wilhelmina of Prussia, and in about 1730 he had been foiled by Walpole in his attempt to marry Lady Diana Spencer. He had

Though Mr. Apshones does not represent any person, he may be a literary burlesque of the tenant Welford in Lillo's ballad opera *Silvia; or, The Country Burial* (1730).[9]

Despite the impudent political burlesque, which would have pleased Walpole's opponents, an examination of *The Grub-Street Opera* does not indicate that Fielding had made a total commitment to the Opposition. The tone of his play is mild compared with that of some of the anti-Walpole literature in circulation at the time. For example, a vituperation entitled *Robin's Panegyrick: or, The Norfolk Miscellany* (1731) asserted that Walpole had the following traits:

> . . . a malicious, vindictive, sanguinary Nature; a saucy insulting, over-bearing, imperious Behaviour in Prosperity; a poor, low, wretched, mean, abject Spirit in Adversity; of a perfidious, impious, atheistical Principle; remarkably addicted to Lying; an ignorant, forward, positive, unexperienc'd, headstrong, blundering Driver; despised, contemned, and hated by all his Master's faithful Servants.
>
> (Vol. II, p. 5)

The tone of this passage is not untypical of other Opposition works which condemned Walpole in every way possible (e.g., for his relationship with Molly Skerrit, the profits he made from South-Sea stock, his use of patronage and bribery, his close relationship with Queen Caroline, his liberality with the civil-list money, his use of the national debt to forsake a pay-as-you-go fiscal policy, his taxation schemes, his secret service, and his desire to keep England at peace [which justified to some the claim that he was a coward]). Although

---

several mistresses, according to the Earl of Egmont; in late 1731 he was keeping an "apothecary's daughter of Kingston," and in 1732 he professed to be the father of a child by Anne Vane, one of Queen Caroline's maids of honor. In *les affairs du coeur*, however, he was apparently "not nice in his choice," and talked more than he acted. Indeed, court gossip had it that Frederick was impotent, a rumor that was later disproved by the number of children, including George III, that he fathered by Augusta, Princess of Saxe-Gotha. But in 1731 Frederick was young and his virility was in question, despite his notorious pursuit of Caroline's maids of honor. See Peter Quennel, *Caroline of England: An Augustan Portrait* (New York, 1940), p. 106; Reginald Lucas, *George II and His Ministers* (London, 1910), p. 46; and the *Diary of the Earl of Egmont*, Historical MSS. Commission, I, 208, 235–236.

9 Ernest Bernbaum, *The Drama of Sensibility* (Cambridge, Mass., 1915), pp. 144 f.

the attacks raised some legitimate political issues, they concentrated mainly on the personality of Walpole. They pictured him allegorically as a principal coachman, a butler, or a steward on a large estate; gave him the names "Bob," "Robin," "Brazen-Face," or "Lyn"; and drew him as a dishonest and dishonorable character who constantly violated his master's trust. Compared with these works, Fielding's play, though subtle, is good-natured.

More noteworthy than Fielding's satire on Walpole and the Ministry is his satire on the royal family. It was most probably this that made the Government particularly anxious to remove the play from public view. The first scene highlights the dissension among the Apshinkens—the royal family—and, though later in the play the plot concerning the servants—Walpole and his government versus the Opposition—is developed at great length, the Apshinken plot is continually important. Fielding's portrait of George II as Sir Owen shows a genial individual but one who deserts his responsibilities and duties, a shortcoming that geniality could not excuse.

Lady Apshinken assumes the governing role that Sir Owen has abandoned, just as Caroline exercised the royal powers by subtly controlling the king's decisions (according to Lord Hervey's *Memoirs*). It was Caroline whom Fielding had in mind when he gave *The Welsh Opera* the subtitle *The Grey Mare the Better Horse*. To Lady Apshinken he attributed no virtues but many faults, including niggardliness, intellectual pretentiousness, hostility to English customs (prompting his most famous song, "When Mighty Roast Beef Was the English-man's Food"), and dissatisfaction with her husband. Nor does his portrait of her ever mellow; it is Lady Apshinken who gracelessly strikes the one note of discord in the merriment ending the play.

If the attack on Caroline is severe, that on Frederick Louis, Prince of Wales, through the character of Master Owen, borders on the scandalous. Both the Welsh setting and the title of the early version centered attention upon the Prince, and in both versions he was portrayed as a beau, in Fielding's writings a recurrent symbol of uselessness and frivolity. Burlesquing the rift in the royal family caused by Frederick's abortive marriage attempts, Fielding created the affair between Molly and Master Owen, and gave Lady Apshinken this comment about Master Owen's stupidity: "Whatever nature hath done for him in another way, she hath left his head unfurnished" (I.ii). The satire grows more severe as the prince's notorious deceitfulness is mocked when Master Owen writes the false letters. Deceitfulness, however, was not the gravest fault, or alleged fault, satirized by Fielding: throughout the play there are many references to Frederick's rumored impotence. Here was scandal. Though George II and Queen Caroline favored their second son William, Duke of Cumberland, and though their dislike of Frederick eventually grew to hatred, nonetheless a literary attack like Fielding's could not be tolerated. Insinuations that the Prince of Wales was unable to further the royal line were potentially so damaging to the reputation of the royal family that *The Grub-Street Opera* could have been construed as an attack upon the institution of the Crown itself.

Fielding not only carried out this burlesque of the royal family in the action of the play, but he continued his mockery in selecting their names. The name *Shenkin*, also spelled *Shinken* and *Shinking*, appeared in a popular song which Fielding selected as the music for Air XXXIV of *The Grub-Street Opera*.[10] The original lyrics, by Thomas D'Urfey, were about a young man named Shenkin, whose "renown" had "fled and gone" after he had been pursued by "cruel Love." This Shenkin was "of noble race"; indeed, he was descended from the "line of Owen Tudor."[11] The King of England and the Prince of Wales were also of this line, since Owen Tudor, a Welsh gentleman of the fifteenth century, was the grandfather of Henry VII, from whom all subsequent British monarchs trace their origins (Fielding's giving the name "Owen" to both the father and son is therefore significant, as is also his laying the scene of the play in Wales). In the association of D'Urfey's original song and Fielding's lyrics (which claim that when the grey mare is the better horse, the horse is "but an ass") there is a profound insult of the royal family. To imply that the King of England was an ass, or to suggest that the "renown" of the royal line of the Welsh Owen Tudor was "fled and gone," was certainly a joke that would have offended the king and his family. Moreover, it is interesting that Fielding's version of the name *Shinken* in *Apshinken* sounds like the German word *Schinken*, which means "a ham." If Fielding intended the name *Shinken* to suggest this meaning, then the

---

[10] Just three years before, the music of this song had been made popular by Gay in *The Beggar's Opera* (Air 31).

[11] The relevant stanza, the first, is as follows: Of noble Race was *Shinking*,/ The Line of *Owen Tudor*,/ *Thum, thum, thum, thum*,/ But her Renown is fled and gone,/ Since cruel Love pursu'd her (Brit. Mus. H. 1601. No. 330).

(Lest confusion arise about the sex of this Shinking, it should be explained that the word *her* in the song was a Welsh dialectal form for *his* and *him*.)

name *Apshinken* would mean "the son of a ham." Though at the time, perhaps, not many Englishmen would have understood the allusion, a reference to the German origin of the royal family seems to be implied.

Clearly Fielding's play is filled with mockery and scorn for Caroline and Frederick. Such a tone, together with his irreverent if not hostile treatment of political figures, easily explains the Ministry's probable role in the removal of *The Grub-Street Opera* from the stage. It also explains why the two early spurious publications of the play were greeted with Governmental repression. Although the entire incident hurt Fielding only slightly—by the next season he had gained an even better theatrical affiliation than he lost—in historical perspective the Governmental action was a step on the way toward the Stage Licensing Act of 1737. From Fielding's point of view, it is as though the fate of *The Grub-Street Opera* was a rehearsal for the termination of his career as a practicing dramatist after his great political satires, *Pasquin* and *The Historical Register*.

Since Fielding's ambitious and audacious ballad opera thus marks his first excursion into the political arena, it has held great interest for his biographers and for students of the drama. The attention usually paid to its topical themes, however, should not obscure the fact that it possesses artistic merit. *The Grub-Street Opera* is typical of Fielding's methods as a dramatist. Like many of his plays, it was written quickly and then revised when it met success; though it relies heavily upon conventional dramatic plots, it is enriched by burlesque and concentrates finally on serious human problems. It is written from a consistently realistic and tolerant point of view: if the characters all have shortcomings, most of them are good-natured in the special way that Tom Jones is good-natured. That is, although a character may make mistakes, he is worth sympathy because of his general sense of rightness and fairness—his good nature, his sense of balance and proportion. Most characters in *The Grub-Street Opera* are shown as interesting and representative human beings.

As a dramatic allegory, the play represents the real political opposition as the dramatic conflict produced between Robin and William by Master Owen's deceptive letters. Trivial as it is, this conflict in turn causes the rift between Robin and Sweetissa, the arguments between Susan and Sweetissa, the fight between Robin and William, and the hostility between Robin and Puzzletext. That the conflict in the servant plot is based on misunderstandings suggests Fielding's scorn for the political entanglements. Hervey, in his *Memoirs*, asserted that the difference between the Government and the Opposition at the time was the difference between "Whigs in place" and "Whigs out of place."[12] Fielding's perspective was similar. Political parties, one must remember, were still relatively new, and the English experience with them had been that they tended to produce unreasonable conflict. Many thoughtful men of the time, Fielding included, believed that men should agree on moral principles (which they frequently identified with the principles of their own party), and consequently felt that party division was not simply a divergence of political method but also a destruction of morality. Swift's *Gulliver's Travels*, for example, contains numerous allusions to the revolutionary danger inherent in a permanent division of the body politic into parties. Similarly, Fielding's representation of the Walpole-Pulteney division implies that men in agreement on moral principles were letting personal differences and petty misunderstandings endanger the country's prospects for continued peace and prosperity. In short, the political situation in Fielding's eyes was muddled by the side issue of personality, and it is precisely this muddling that he satirized in *The Grub-Street Opera*.

When seen in this perspective, *The Grub-Street Opera* is a significant political commentary, but it may also be seen in general, human terms. The title, with its reference to Grub Street, serves by analogy to connect the play's action with much of human life. Grub Street was of course the traditional home of literary hacks, whom Fielding had satirized in *The Author's Farce*. *The Grub-Street Opera*, however, is only secondarily a literary attack. Through the character of "Scriblerus Secundus" in the Introduction, Fielding declared his intention to expose what he called Grub-Street "wit": "Ah, ah, the whole wit of Grub Street consists in these two little words—*you lie.*" He went further to say, as "Scriblerus Secundus," that

> I believe I am the first that hath attempted to introduce this sort of wit upon the stage, but it hath flourished among our political members a long while. Nay, in short, it is the only wit that flourishes among them.

Grub-Street "wit," in Fielding's eyes, was neither intelligent nor

[12] John, Lord Hervey, *Some Materials Towards Memoirs of the Reign of King George the Second*, ed. Romney Sedgwick (London, 1931), I, 4.

comic; it was an inability or deliberate refusal to examine issues clearly, to determine truth, and to act upon it. Another definition of this wit, or witlessness, might be the turning away from self-knowledge. In this larger sense, the play attributes such witlessness not only to politicians but to society at all levels (fine gentlemen, servants, young gentlemen attempting seduction, newlyweds, people of quality who see only surface virtues, persons who rationalize failure, stingy persons who profess economy, and hypocritical preachers, all of whom appear or are mentioned in the play). Grub-Street wit is all-pervasive and potentially destructive in society, though at the beginning at least its action is subtle. It is such wit that has given Master Owen a misguided sense of his own worth. Similarly, failures of insight make it possible for Sir Owen to neglect his proprietary role and for Lady Apshinken to assume it; all the rest of the characters make mistakes when their own anger or personal loyalties prevent them from examining the truth in order to determine whether they are acting rightly. Men everywhere, in other words, deceive themselves first and consequently can do little better than deceive their fellow human beings. In this sense, Fielding's play successfully exposes Grub-Street "wit." His development of his theme is a powerful reminder of how his mind worked toward generality, for his first version of the play, *The Welsh Opera*, was a period piece exposing the follies of current politics; his second version, *The Grub-Street Opera*, was built upon the first with the addition of general satire developing the symbol of mankind's bent toward self-deception.

His generally satirical purpose was therefore already true to the principle he was to pursue in *Joseph Andrews* and *Tom Jones*, and in this early play, as in his mature works, he did not allow the serious burden of his criticism to overbalance his comic tone. In Air XI, for example, Sweetissa sings of her love for Robin in words reminiscent of the refrain of "Johnny Shall Have a New Bonnet," a poem which has since become a standard nursery rhyme; at the play's end Fielding recaptures this mood by having his characters exit to the music of "Little Jack Horner." These suggestions of a childish world—as well as the allegory of the piece, the attention given to self-deception, and the attempt to achieve a proverbial quality (both through already-existing proverbs and through those that Fielding made his characters speak for the first time)—put the play on a level somewhat removed from immediate reality. Fielding's primary intention to amuse is thereby underscored, and the reader is also invited to see the squabbles among the characters (and their real-life analogues) as unreal and insignificant, of no importance or permanence. The play thus cautions men to avoid the Grub-Street error of "you lie," and to learn to find reality and truth in human affairs. Without such self-awareness, Fielding implies, human beings behave like children whose world is governed by fairy tales.

I should like to express my thanks to Miss Elaine Lisinsky, who lent her musical knowledge to the careful preparation of the music for the press (Appendix C), and to Mrs. Frances Woods, for her kindness in permitting me to use the notes and microfilm of her late husband, Professor Charles B. Woods. For financial assistance I am grateful to the United States Fulbright Scholarship Program, the American Council of Learned Societies, and the Nora and Abbie Fund of Hunter College.

EDGAR V. ROBERTS

Hunter College in the Bronx
(Herbert H. Lehman College after July, 1968)
of The City University of New York

THE GRUB-STREET OPERA

Sing. Nom. *Hic, Haec, Hoc.*
Gen. *Hujus.*
Dat. *Huic.*
Accus. *Hunc, Hanc, Hoc.*
Voc. *Caret.*
—Lil. Gram. quod vid.

The epigraph is from the section "Articles" in William Lily's *A Short Introduction to Grammar*, which had been a standard Latin grammar since 1540 (see the edition with an introduction by Vincent J. Flynn [New York, 1945], p. x).

INTRODUCTION

Scriblerus, Player.

PLAYER.

I very much approve the alteration of your title from the
Welsh to the *Grub-Street Opera*.

SCRIBLERUS.

I hope, sir, it will recommend me to that learned society, for
they like nothing but what is most indisputably their own.

PLAYER.

I assure you it recommends you to me, and will, I hope, to   5
the town.

SCRIBLERUS.

It would be impolitic in you, who are a young beginner, to
oppose that society, which the established theaters so pro-
fessedly favor. Besides, you see the town are ever on its side,
for I would not have you think, sir, all the members of that   10
august body confined to the street they take their name from.
No, no, the rules of Grub Street are as extensive as the rules
of the King's Bench. We have them of all orders and degrees,
and it is no more a wonder to see our members in ribbands
than to see them in rags.   15

PLAYER.

May the whole society unite in your favor.

SCRIBLERUS.

Nay, sir, I think no man can set out with greater assurance
of success. It was the favor which the town hath already
shown to *The Welsh Opera* which gave birth to this, wherein
I have kept only what they particularly approved in the   20
former. You will find several additions to the first act, the
second and third, except in one scene, entirely new.

12–13. *the rules . . . Bench*] Prisoners committed to the King's Bench
Prison in Southwark for debt were, upon payment of a fee (prisons at the
time were privately operated as a concession), allowed the freedom of
residing within a prescribed area outside the prison. This area was called
the *rules*, or liberties, of the King's Bench. Frequently, however, prisoners
ignored the rules and lived wherever they pleased, thus extending the rules
far beyond the legally defined perimeter (Walter Thornbury and Edward
Walford, *Old and New London* [London, 1897], VI, 64 f.).

PLAYER.

You have made additions indeed to the altercative or scolding scenes, as you are pleased to call them.

SCRIBLERUS.

Oh, sir, they cannot be heightened; too much altercation 25
is the particular property of Grub Street. With what spirit
do Robin and Will rap out the lie at one another for half a
page together—you lie, and you lie. Ah, ah, the whole wit
of Grub Street consists in these two little words—*you lie*.

PLAYER.

That is esteemed so unanswerable a repartee, that it is 30
among gentlemen generally the last word that is spoken.

SCRIBLERUS.

Ay, sir, and it is the first and last among ours. I believe I am
the first that hath attempted to introduce this sort of wit
upon the stage, but it hath flourished among our political
members a long while. Nay, in short, it is the only wit that 35
flourishes among them.

PLAYER.

And may you get as much by it as they do. But pray, sir,
what is the plot or design of this opera? For I could not well
discover at the rehearsals.

SCRIBLERUS.

As for plot, sir, I had writ an admirable one; but having 40
observed that the plot of our English operas have had no
good effect on our audiences, so I have e'en left it out. For
the design, it is deep, very deep. This opera was writ, sir,
with a design to instruct the world in economy. It is a sort of
family opera—the husband's *vade mecum*—and is very neces- 45
sary for all married men to have in their houses. So if you
please I will communicate a word or two of my design to the
audience, while you prepare matters behind the scenes.

PLAYER.

I shall expect you there, sir.   [*Exit.*]

SCRIBLERUS.

The author does in humble scenes produce   50
Examples fitted to your private use.
Teaches each man to regulate his life,

45. *vade mecum*] *made macum GSO.*

To govern well his servants and his wife;
Teaches that servants will their masters chouse,
That wives will ride their husbands round the house; 55
Teaches that jealousy does oft arise,
Because men's sense is dimmer than their eyes;
Teaches young gentlemen do oft pursue
More women than they well know how to—woo;
Teaches that parsons teach us the right way, 60
And when we err we mind not what they say;
Teaches that pious women often groan
For sake of their religion—when they've none;
Teaches that virtue is the maid's best store;
Teaches all these, and teaches nothing more.   [*Exit.*] 65

---

54. *chouse*] "to dupe, cheat, trick; to swindle or defraud *of* or *out of*" (*OED*).

DRAMATIS PERSONAE

Men

SIR OWEN APSHINKEN, a gentlemen of Wales, in love with tobacco	*Mr. Furnival*
MASTER OWEN APSHINKEN, his son, in love with womankind	*Mr. Stoppelaer*
MR. APSHONES, his tenant	*Mr. Wathan*
PUZZLETEXT, his chaplain, in love with women, tobacco, drink and backgammon	*Mr. Reynolds*
ROBIN, his butler, in love with Sweetissa	*Mr. Mullart*
WILLIAM, his coachman, enemy to Robin, in love with Susan	*Mr. Jones*
JOHN, his groom, in love with Margery	*Mr. Dove*
THOMAS, the gardener	*Mr. Hicks*

Women

LADY APSHINKEN, wife to Sir Owen, a great housewife, governante to her husband, a zealous advocate for the Church	*Mrs. Furnival*
MOLLY APSHONES, daughter to Mr. Apshones, a woman of strict virtue	*Miss Patty Vaughan*

SWEETISSA, waiting woman ⎫
SUSAN, cook   ⎬ *Women of strict virtue, in love with*
MARGERY, housemaid   ⎭

⎧ Robin ⎫ *Mrs. Nokes*
⎨ Will ⎬ *Mrs. Mullart*
⎩ John ⎭ *Mrs. Lacy*

Scene: *Wales, North or South*

Sir Owen Apshinken] The "Ap" is a Welsh equivalent of "son" or "Mac." The common English equivalent of "Shinken" or "Shenkin" is "Jenkin" or "Jenkins."

Mr. Apshones] The common English equivalent of "Shones" is "Jones."

Puzzletext] Fielding may have borrowed this name from Charles Coffey's *Female Parson*, a short-lived ballad opera first performed on April 27, 1730, at the New Theatre in the Haymarket. In the relevant passage (Act III), the character Sir Quibble greets the disguised maid, Pinner, as follows: ". . . welcome, welcome, my dear *Puzzletext*, . . ."

The Grub-Street Opera

ACT I

[I.i]   *Scene, Sir Owen Apshinken's House. Table and Chairs.*
Sir Owen Apshinken and Puzzletext, smoking.

SIR OWEN.

Come, Mr. Puzzletext, it is your glass. Let us make an end
of our breakfast before Madam is up. Oh, Puzzletext, what
a fine thing it is for a man of my estate to stand in fear of his
wife, that I dare not get drunk so much as—once a day,
without being called to an account for it.   5

PUZZLETEXT.

Petticoat government is a very lamentable thing indeed.
But it is the fate of many an honest gentleman.

AIR I [*A Lusty Young Smith*]

What a wretched life
Leads a man a tyrant wife,
While for each small fault he's corrected: 10
One bottle makes a sot,
One girl is ne'er forgot,
And duty is always neglected.
But though nothing can be worse
Than this fell domestic curse,   15
Some comfort this may do you,
So vast are the hen-pecked bands,
That each neighbor may shake hands,
With my humble service to you.

7.1. *A Lusty Young Smith*]   *WO,*
GGSO; not in GSO.

The Grub-Street Opera] The title may have been suggested by the following
passage in Tony Aston's *Fool's Opera* (published April 1, 1731), p. 2:
"*Poet.* Sirrah, you're not so great a Fool as you would make yourself.
Fool. Nor you so great a Wit, for all you wrote the Original *Grub-street*
Opera, Cudden. *Poet.* I have published the sequel at Six Shillings a-piece."

SIR OWEN.

Oh, Puzzletext, if I could but enjoy my pipe undisturbed,   20
how happy should I be! For I never yet could taste any
pleasure, but in tobacco.

PUZZLETEXT.

Tobacco is a very good thing, indeed, and there is no harm
in taking it abundantly.

[I.ii]   Sir Owen Apshinken, Lady Apshinken, Puzzletext.

LADY APSHINKEN.

At your morning-draught, Sir Owen, I find, according to
custom; but I shall not trouble myself with such a drone as
you are. Methinks you, Mr. Puzzletext, should not encour-
age drunkenness.

PUZZLETEXT.

I ask your ladyship's pardon. I profess I have scarce drank   5
your health this morning. And wine, while it contributeth
only to the cheering of the spirits, is not forbidden us. I am
an enemy to excess, but as far as the second bottle—nay, to
some constitutions, a third—it is, no doubt, allowable. And
I do remember to have preached with much perspicuity   10
even after a fourth.

LADY APSHINKEN.

Oh intolerable! Do you call four bottles no excess?

PUZZLETEXT.

To some it may, to others it may not. Excess dependeth not
on the quantity that is drank, but on the quality of him who
drinketh.   15

LADY APSHINKEN.

I do not understand this sophistry, though I think I have
some skill in divinity—

PUZZLETEXT.

Oh, madam, no one more. Your ladyship is the honor of
your sex in that study, and may properly be termed "the
great Welsh lamp of divinity."   20

9. it] *GGSO, WO; not in GSO.*

19–20. *the great . . . divinity*] Queen Caroline was an amateur theologian
of some ability (Cross, I, 106).

LADY APSHINKEN.

I have always had an inclination to maintain religion in the parish, and some other time should be very glad to dispute with you concerning excess. But at present I must impart something to you concerning my son, whom I have observed too familiar with the maids. 25

PUZZLETEXT.

Which of the maids, madam?—(*Aside.*) Not one of my mistresses, I hope.

LADY APSHINKEN.

Truly, with all of them. And unless we prevent it, I am afraid we shall hear of a marriage not much to our liking. And you know, Mr. Puzzletext, how hard a thing it would 30 be for us, who have but one child, to have him throw himself away.

PUZZLETEXT.

What methods shall we take in order thereto?

LADY APSHINKEN.

I know but one: we must prevent his marrying them, by marrying them to others. We have as many men as maids; 35 now I rely on you to match them up to one another, for whilst there is one unmarried wench in the house I shall think him in danger. Oh, Mr. Puzzletext, the boy takes after his father, not me. His head is full of nothing but love; for whatever nature hath done for him in another way, she 40 hath left his head unfurnished.

PUZZLETEXT.

Love, in a young mind, is powerful indeed.

AIR II, *Lads of Dunce*

If love gets into a soldier's heart,
He puts off his helmet, his bow, and his dart.
Achilles, charmed with a nymph's fair eye, 45
A distaff took, and his arms laid by.
The gay gods of old their heav'n would quit,
And leave their ambrosia for a mortal titbit;
The first of that tribe, that whoremaster Jove,
Preferred to all heav'ns, the heaven of love. 50

LADY APSHINKEN.

I think you have already asked them all in the church, so

that you have only to hasten the match. This I assure you, I
shall not forget the favor. I am now going to take a short
airing in the park, in my own chaise, and would have you
remember we have no time to lose.   [*Exit.*]   55

PUZZLETEXT.

Well, sir, you heard what my lady says. What shall I do?

SIR OWEN.

E'en what she commands. If she interferes not with my pipe,
I am resolved not to interfere with her family. Let her
govern, while I smoke.   [*Exit.*]

PUZZLETEXT.

Upon my word, Sir Owen is a thorough Epicurean philos-   60
opher. I must now seek the young squire, who is a
philosopher of another kind.   [*Exit.*]

[I.iii]   Owen, *solus, with two letters.*

OWEN.

This is the day wherein Robin and Sweetissa propose to be
married, which unless I can prevent, I lose all my hopes of
her; for when once a woman knows what's what, she knows
too much for me. Sure never man was so put to it in his
amours, for I do not care to venture on a woman after   5
another, nor does any woman care for me twice.

AIR III, *Let the Drawer Bring Clean Glasses*

How curst the puny lover!
How exquisite the pain,
When love is fumbled over,
    To view the fair's disdain!   10
But oh, how vast the blessing,
Whom to her bosom pressing,
She whispers, while caressing,
    Oh, when shall we again?

Here are two letters, which I have forged—one as from   15
Susan to Robin, the other from William to Sweetissa.

55. S.D. *Exit*] *WO, GGSO; not in*   *GSO.*
GSO.   62. S.D. *Exit*] *WO; not in GGSO,*
59. S.D. *Exit*] *WO, GGSO; not in*   *GSO.*

These must be dropped where they may be found by the improper parties, and will create a jealousy, whereof I may reap the fruit, and Sweetissa's maidenhead may be yet my own.   20

[I.iv]   Puzzletext *and* Owen

PUZZLETEXT.

Mr. Owen, I have been searching you. I am come, child, to give you some good instructions. I am sorry to hear you have an intention to disgrace your family, by a marriage inferior to your birth.

OWEN.

Do not trouble your head with my marriage, good Mr.   5
Parson. When I marry, 'twill be to please myself, not you.

PUZZLETEXT.

But let it not be such a marriage as may reflect upon your understanding. Consider, sir, consider who you are.

AIR IV, *March in Scipio*

Think, mighty sir, ere you are undone,
Think who you are, Apshinken's only son;   10
At Oxford you have been, at London eke also;
You're almost half a man, and more than half a beau:
Oh do not then disgrace the great actions of your life!
Nor let Apshinken's son be buried in his wife.

You must govern your passions, Master Owen.   15

OWEN.

You may preach, Mr. Parson, but I shall very little regard you. There is nothing so ridiculous as to hear an old fellow railing at love.

PUZZLETEXT.

It is like a young fellow's railing at age.

OWEN.

Or a courtier out of place at court.   20

AIR V, *Sir Thomas I Cannot*

The worn-out rake at pleasure rails,
And cries, 'tis all idle and fleeting;

At court, the man whose int'rest fails,
  Cries, all is corruption and cheating:
    But would you know   25
    Whence both these flow,
  Though so much they pretend to abhor them?
    That rails at court,
    This at love's sport,
  Because they are neither fit for 'em,   30
        fit for 'em,
  Because they are neither fit for 'em.

Besides, Doctor, I fancy you have not always governed your
own passions, though you are so fond of correcting others, as
a poet burlesques the nonsense of others, while he writes   35
greater nonsense himself.

PUZZLETEXT.

Or as a prude corrects the vices of others, while she is more
vicious herself.

OWEN.

Or as a parson preaches against drinking, and then goes to
the alehouse.   40

PUZZLETEXT.

Very true, if you mean a Presbyterian parson.

AIR VI, *One Evening Having Lost My Way*

I've heard a noncon parson preach
  'Gainst whoring, with just disdain;
Whilst he himself to be naught did teach
  Of females as large a train   45
As stars in the sky, or lamps in the street,
Or beauties in the Mall we meet,
    Or as—or as—or as,
  Or as whores in Drury Lane.

OWEN.

Thy similes are all froth, like bottled ale; and it is as difficult 50
to get thee out of a simile as out of an alehouse.

AIR VII, *Dutch Skipper*

PUZZLETEXT. The gaudy sun adorning
        With brightest rays the morning,
              the morning,

Shines o'er the eastern hill;   55
And I will go a-sporting,
OWEN.   And I will go a-courting,
                    a-courting,
There lies my pleasure still.
PUZZLETEXT.   In Gaffer Woodford's ground,   60
A brushing hare is found,
A course which even kings themselves might see;
OWEN.   And in another place
There lies a brushing lass,
Which will give one ten times more sport than   65
she.

Second Part

PUZZLETEXT.   What pleasure to see, while the greyhounds are
                    running,
Poor puss's cunning, and shifting, and shunning!
To see with what art she plays still her part,
And leaves her pursuers afar:
First this way, then that;   70
First a stretch, and then squat,
Till quite out of breath,
She yields her to death.
What joys with the sportsman's compare?

OWEN.   How sweet to behold the soft blooming lass,   75
With blushing face, clasped close in embrace!
To feel her breasts rise, see joy fill her eyes,
And glout on her heav'n of charms!
While sighing and whining,
And twisting and twining,   80
With kissing and pressing,
And fondest caressing,
With raptures she dies in your arms.   *Exeunt.*

74. joys] *WO, GGSO;* joy *GSO.*

61. *brushing*] "Having a brushing tail" (*OED*). Among hunters, a *brush*
was a fox's tail (Bailey).
78. *glout*] i.e., glut, "to feed to repletion; to indulge . . . to the utmost"
(*OED*).

[I.v]   Sweetissa *and* Margery.

SWEETISSA.

If ever you had known what it was to love, Margery, you
would not have wondered how I could prefer a man to his
master.

MARGERY.

I should not have wondered indeed, if our young squire had
been like most young country squires. But he is a fine   5
gentleman, Sweetissa.

SWEETISSA.

From such fine gentlemen may my stars deliver me,
Margery.

MARGERY.

What, I suppose you are afraid of being made jealous by his
running after other women.   10

SWEETISSA.

Pshaw! I should not think him worth being jealous of. He
runs after every woman he sees, and yet, I believe, scarce
knows what a woman is. Either he has more affectation than
desire, or more desire than capacity. Oh Margery, when I
was in London with Madam, I have seen several such   15
sparks as these; some of them would attempt making love
too. Nay, I have had such lovers! But I could never find one
of them that would stand it out.

AIR VIII, *Bessy Bell and Mary Gray*

In long pigtails and shining lace,
        Our beaux set out a-wooing;   20
Ye widows, never show them grace,
        But laugh at their pursuing.
But let the daw, that shines so bright,
        Of borrowed plumes bereft be,
Alas, poor dame, how naked the sight!   25
        You'll find there's nothing left ye.

Oh Margery, there is more in Robin's little finger than in a
beau's whole body.

MARGERY.

Yes, and more roguery in him than—

SWEETISSA.

I know you are prejudiced against him from what William   30

says; but be assured that is all malice; he is desirous of
getting his place.

MARGERY.

I rather think that a prejudice of yours against William.

SWEETISSA.

Oh Margery, Margery, an upper servant's honesty is never
so conspicuous as when he is abused by the under servants.   35
They must rail at someone, and if they abuse him, he
preserves his master and mistress from abuse.

MARGERY.

Well, I would not have such a sweetheart.

SWEETISSA.

Puh! If all you say were true, what is it to me? If women
were to consider the roguery of their lovers, we should have   40
even fewer matches among people of quality than we have.

AIR IX, *Mad Moll*

Why should not I love Robin?
  And why should not Bob love me?
While ev'ry one else he is fobbing,
  He still may be honest to me.   45
For though his master he cheats,
  His mistress shares what he gains;
And whilst I am tasting the sweets,
  The devil take her who complains.

MARGERY.   But should he be taken indeed;   50
  Ah! think what a shame it would be
To have your love dragged out of bed,
  And thence in a cart to the tree.

SWEETISSA.   Let halters tie up the poor cheat,
  Who only deserves to be banged;   55
The wit who can get an estate,
  Hath still too much wit to be hanged.

But I don't speak this on Robin's account! For if all my
master's ancestors had met with as good servants as Robin,
he had enjoyed a better estate than he hath now.   60

[*Exit* Margery.]

61. S.D. *Exit* Margery] *not in WO,*
GGSO, GSO.

–15–

[I.vi]   Robin *and* Sweetissa.

                        AIR X, *Masquerade Minuet.*

ROBIN.   Oh my Sweetissa!
                Give me a kiss-a,
                Oh what a bliss-a
                To behold your charms!
                My eyes with gazing   5
                Are set a-blazing.
SWEETISSA.   Come then and quench them within my arms.
ROBIN.

Oh my Sweetissa, thou art straighter than the straightest
tree, sweeter than the sweetest flower. Thy hand is white as
milk, and as warm; thy breast is as white as snow, and as   10
cold. Thou art, to sum thee up at once, an olio of perfections;
or in other words, a garden of bliss which my soul delights
to walk in. Oh, I will take such strides about thy form, such
vast, such mighty strides—

SWEETISSA.

Oh Robin, it is as impossible to tell thee how much I love   15
thee, as it is to tell—how much water there is in the sea.

ROBIN.

My dear Sweetissa, had I the learning of the author of that
opera book in the parlor window, I could not make a simile
to my love.

SWEETISSA.

Be assured there shall be no love lost between us.   20

                AIR XI, *Young Damon Once the Happiest Swain*

                When mutual passion hath possessed,
                With equal flame, each amorous breast,
                    How sweet's the rapt'rous kiss!
                While each with soft contention strive,
                Which highest ecstasies shall give,   25
                    Or be more mad with bliss.

---

18. *simile*] A convention of Italian operas of the time was the so-called
"simile song"; that is, a lyric which developed a simile or metaphor throughout its length. See, for example, "I'm like a vessel on the main" in *Faramondo*
(1737), by Zeno, music by Handel, Act II, scene viii.

ROBIN.

Oh my Sweetissa, how impatient am I till the parson hath stitched us together; then, my dear, nothing but the scissors of the Fates should ever cut us asunder.

SWEETISSA.

How charming is thy voice! sweeter than bagpipes to my ear. I could listen ever. 30

ROBIN.

And I could view thee ever; thy face is brighter than the brightest silver. Oh could I rub my silver to be as bright as thy dear face, I were a butler indeed!

SWEETISSA.

Oh Robin, there is no rubbing on my face. The color which 35 I have, Nature, not art, hath given; for on my honor, during the whole time I have lived with my mistress, out of all the pots of paint which I have plaistered on her face, I never stole a bit to plaister on my own.

ROBIN.

Adieu, my dear. I must go whet my knives. By that time the 40 parson will be returned from coursing, and we will be married this morning. Oh, Sweetissa, it is easier to fathom the depth of the bottomless sea than my love.

SWEETISSA.

Or to fathom the depth of a woman's bottomless conscience than to tell thee mine. 45

ROBIN.

Mine is as deep as the knowledge of physicians.

SWEETISSA.

Mine as the projects of statesmen.

ROBIN.

Mine as the virtue of whores.

SWEETISSA.

Mine as the honesty of lawyers.

ROBIN.

Mine as the piety of priests. 50

SWEETISSA.

Mine as—I know not what.

ROBIN.

Mine as—as—as—I'gad I don't know what.

While the symphony is playing, Robin *pulls out a handkerchief,*
blows his nose, and drops a letter.

AIR XII, *All in the Downs*

Would you my love in words displayed,
A language must be coined to tell,
No word for such a passion's made,   55
For no one ever loved so well.
Nothing, oh nothing's like my love for you,
And so my dearest, and so my dearest, and my dear,
    adieu.   [*Exit.*]

[I.vii]   Sweetissa *and* Margery.

SWEETISSA.

Oh my Margery, if this fit of love continues, how happy
shall I be!

MARGERY.

Ay, it will continue the usual time, I warrant you, during
the honeymoon.

SWEETISSA.

Call it the honey-year, the honey-age. Oh Margery, sure   5
never woman loved as I do. Though I am to be married this
morning, still it seems long to me. To a mind in love, sure
an hour before marriage seems a month.

MARGERY.

Ay, my dear, and many an hour after marriage seems a
twelvemonth; it is the only thing wherein the two states agree,   10
for we generally wish ourselves into it, and wish ourselves
out of it.

SWEETISSA.

And then into it again, which makes one poet say love is
like the wind.

MARGERY.

Another, that it is like the sea.   15

SWEETISSA.

A third, a weathercock.

52.1. *While . . . letter*] *WO; not in*   58.1. *Exit*] *WO; not in GGSO, GSO.*
GGSO, GSO.

-18-

MARGERY.

A fourth, a Jack with a lanthorn.

SWEETISSA.

In short, it is like everything.

MARGERY.

And like nothing at all.

AIR XIII, *Ye Nymphs and Sylvan Gods*

How odd a thing is love, 20
Which the poets fain would prove
To be this and that,
And the Lord knows what,
Like all things below and above.
But believe a maid, 25
Skilled enough in the trade
Its mysteries to explain;
'Tis a gentle dart,
That tickles the heart,
And though it gives us smart, 30
Does joys impart,
Which largely requite all the pain.

MARGERY.

Oh, my dear, whilst you have been singing, see what I have
discovered.   [*She gives* Sweetissa *a letter*.]

SWEETISSA.

It is a woman's hand, and not my own. (*Reads.*) Oh my 35
Margery, now I am undone indeed. Robin is false; he has
lain with, and left, our Susan.

MARGERY.

How?

SWEETISSA.

This letter comes from her, to upbraid him with it.

MARGERY.

Then you have reason to thank fate for this timely discovery. 40

33. S.D. *She ... letter*] *not in WO,*
GGSO, GSO.

17. *Jack with a lanthorn*] an *ignis fatuus*, a will-o'-the-wisp; not the American
Jack-o'-lantern.

–19–

What would it avail you to have found it out when you were
married to him? When you had been his wife, what would
it have profited you to have known he had another?

SWEETISSA.

True, true, Margery, when once a woman is married, 'tis
too late to discover faults.   45

AIR XIV, *Red House*

Ye virgins who would marry,
Ere you choose, be wary,
If you'd not miscarry,
Be inclined to doubting:
Examine well your lover,   50
His vices to discover,
With caution con him over,
And turn quite inside out him;
But wedding past,
The stocking cast,   55
The guests all gone,
The curtain drawn,
Be henceforth blind,
Be very kind,
And find no faults about him.   60

SWEETISSA.

Oh Margery, I am resolved never to see Robin more.

MARGERY.

Keep that resolution, and you will be happy.

[*Exeunt.*] Sweetissa *drops a letter.*

[I.viii]   Robin.

ROBIN.

How truly does the book say, hours to men in love are years.
Oh for a shower of rain to send the parson home from
coursing before the canonical hours are over! Ha! What
paper is this? The hand of our William is on the super-
scription.   [*He reads.*]   5

62.1. *Exeunt . . . letter.*] Sweetissa   [I.viii]
drops a letter. WO; not in GGSO,   5. S.D. *He reads.*] *not in WO, GGSO,*
GSO.   *GSO.*

To Mrs. Sweetissa.

Madam,

  Hoping that you are not quite de-t-e-r-ter-m-i-n-e-d, deter-
  mined to marry our Robin, this comes for to let you know—
I'll read no more. Can there be such falsehood in mankind?   10
I find footmen are as great rogues as their masters; and
henceforth I'll look for no more honesty under a livery than
an embroidered coat. But let me see again.   [*He reads again.*]
  —to let you know I am ready to fulfill my promise to you.
Ha! She too is guilty. Chambermaids are as bad as their   15
ladies, and the whole world is one nest of rogues.

AIR XV, *Black Joke*

The more we know of human kind,
The more deceits and tricks you'll find
  In every land as well as Wales;
For would you see no roguery thrive,
Upon the mountains you must live   20
  For rogues abound in all the vales.
The master and the man will nick,
The mistress and the maid will trick;
  For rich and poor   25
  Are rogue and whore,
There's not one honest man in a score,
Nor woman true in twenty-four.

[I.ix]   Robin *and* John.

ROBIN.

Oh John, thou best of friends, come to my arms. For thy
sake I will still believe there is one honest—one honest man
in the world.

JOHN.

What means our Robin?

ROBIN.

Oh my friend, Sweetissa is false, and I'm undone. Let this   5
letter explain the rest.

13. S.D. *He reads again.*] *not in WO,*
GGSO, GSO.

JOHN.

Ha! And is William at the bottom of all? Our William, who
used to rail against women and matrimony. Oh, 'tis too true
what our parson says, there's no belief in man.

ROBIN.

Nor woman either. —John, art thou my friend?   10

JOHN.

When did Robin ask me what I have not done? Have I not
left my horses undressed, to whet thy knives? Have I not
left my stable uncleaned, to clean thy spoons? And even the
bay stonehorse unwatered, to wash thy glasses?

ROBIN.

Then thou shalt carry a challenge for me to William.   15

JOHN.

Oh Robin, consider what our parson says: We must not
revenge, but forget and forgive.

ROBIN.

Let our parson say what he will. When did he himself
forgive? Did he forgive gaffer Jobson having wronged him
of two cocks of hay in five load? Did he forgive gammer   20
Sowgrunt for having wronged him of a tythe-pig? Did he
forgive Susan Foulmouth for telling him he loved the cellar
better than his pulpit? No, no, let him preach up forgiveness; he forgives nobody. So I will follow his example, not
his precepts. Had he hit me a slap in the face, I could have 25
put it up. Had he stole a silver spoon, and laid the blame on
me, though I had been turned away, I could have forgiven
him. But to try to rob me of my love—that, that, our John,
I never can forgive him.

AIR XVI, *Tipling John*

The dog his bit   30
Will often quit,
A battle to eschew;
The cock his corn
Will leave in barn,
Another cock in view.   35

9. parson]   *WO*, *GGSO*;   person
GSO.

One man will eat
Another's meat,
And no contention seen;
Since all agree
'Tis best to be   40
Though hungry, in a whole skin.

But should each spy
His mistress by
A rival move his suit,
He quits his fears,   45
And by the ears,
They fall together to't.
A rival shocks
Men, dogs, and cocks,
And makes the gentlest froward;   50
He who won't fight
For mistress bright
Is something worse than coward.

JOHN.

Nay, to say the truth, thou hast reason on thy side. Fare
thee well. I'll go deliver thy message, and thou shalt find I   55
will behave myself like a Welshman, and thy friend.   [*Exit.*]

[I.x]   Robin.

ROBIN.

Now were it not for the sin of self-murder, would I go hang
myself at the next tree. Yes, Sweetissa, I would hang myself,
and haunt thee. —Oh woman, woman, is this the return
you make true love? No man is sure of his mistress till he
has gotten her with child. A lover should act like a boy at   5
school, who spits in his porridge that no one may take it
from him. Should William have been beforehand with me.
Oh!

56. *Exit*] *not in WO, GGSO, GSO.*   [I.x]
                                             6. spits] *GGSO, GSO;* shits *WO.*

[I.xi]   Robin *and* Sweetissa.

SWEETISSA.

Oh, the perjury of men! I find dreams do not always go by contraries; for I dreamt last night that I saw our Robin married to another.

A long silence, and walking by one another. She takes out her handkerchief, and bursts out a-crying.

ROBIN.

Your crying won't do, madam; I can tell you that. I have been your fool long enough. I have been cheated by your   5 tears too often to believe them any longer.

SWEETISSA.

Oh barbarous, perfidious, cruel wretch! Oh, I shall break my heart! Oh!

ROBIN.

No, no, your heart is like a green stick; you may bend it, but cannot break it. It will bend like a willow, and twist   10 round anyone.

SWEETISSA.

Monster! Monster!

ROBIN.

Better language would show better breeding.

AIR XVII, *Hedge Lane*

Indeed, my dear,
With sigh and tear,   15
Your point you will not carry;
I'd rather eat
The offal meat,
Than others' leavings marry.

SWEETISSA.   Villain, well   20
You would conceal
Your falsehood by such catches;
Alas! too true
I've been to you,
Thou very wretch of wretches.   25
Well you know
What I might do,
Would I but with young master.

ROBIN.   Pray be still,
                    Since by our Will,   30
                    You're now with child of bastard.
SWEETISSA.   I with child?
ROBIN.   Yes, you with child;
SWEETISSA.   I with child, you villain?
ROBIN.   Yes, you,   35
                    Madam, you,
                    Are now with child by William.
    It is equal to me with whom you play your pranks; and I'd
    as leave be my master's cuckold, as my fellow servant's.
    Nay, I had rather, for I could make him pay for it.   40

SWEETISSA.
    Oh most inhuman! Dost thou not expect the ceiling to fall
    down on thy head, for so notorious a lie? Dost thou believe
    in the Bible? Dost thou believe there is such a thing as the
    devil? Dost thou believe there is such a place as hell?

ROBIN.
    Yes, I do, madam; and you will find there is such a place to 45
    your cost. Oh Sweetissa, Sweetissa, that a woman could
    hear herself asked in church to one man, when she knew she
    had to do with another.

SWEETISSA.
    I had to do with another?

ROBIN.
    You, madam, you.   50

SWEETISSA.
    I had to do with Will?

ROBIN.
    Yes, you had to do with Will.

AIR XVIII, *Lord Biron's Maggot*

SWEETISSA.   Sure naught so disastrous can woman befall,
             As to be a good virgin, and thought none at all.
                 Had William but pleased me,   55
                 It never had teased me
             To hear a forsaken man bawl.
                 But from you this abuse,
                 For whose sake, and whose use,

I have safe corked my maidenhead up; 60
How must it shock my ear!
For what woman can bear
To be called a vile drunkard,
And told of the tankard,
Before she has swallowed a cup. 65

ROBIN.

O Sweetissa, Sweetissa! Well thou knowest that wert thou true, I'd not have sold thee for five hundred pounds. But why do I argue longer with an ungrateful woman, who is not only false, but triumphs in her falsehood, her falsehood to one who hath been too true to her. Since you can be so 70 base, I shall tell you what I never did intend to tell you: when I was in London, I might have had an affair with a lady, and slighted her for you.

SWEETISSA.

A lady! I might have had three lords in one afternoon; nay, more than that, I refused a man with a thing over his 75 shoulder like a scarf, at a burying, for you; and these men, they say, are the greatest men in the kingdom.

ROBIN.

Oh Sweetissa, the very hand-irons thou didst rub before thou wast preferred to wait on thy lady, have not more brass in them than thy forehead. 80

SWEETISSA.

Oh Robin, Robin, the great silver candlesticks in thy custody are not more hollow than thou art.

ROBIN.

Oh Sweetissa, the paint, nay, the eyebrows that thou puttest on thy mistress are not more false than thou.

SWEETISSA.

Thou hast as many mistresses as there are glasses on thy 85 sideboard.

ROBIN.

And thou lovers, as thy mistress has patches.

66. Well thou] *GGSO;* well, thou
WO, GSO.

75–76. *thing . . . scarf*] a ceremonial item of apparel distinguishing a man belonging to one of the knightly orders, obviously of the highest social status.

SWEETISSA.

If I have, you will have but a small share.

ROBIN.

The better my fortune. To lose a wife when you have had
her is to get out of misfortune. To lose one before you get   90
her is to escape it, especially if it be one that somebody has
had before you. He that marries pays the price of virtue.
Whores are to be had cheaper.

AIR XIX, *Do Not Ask Me*

A woman's ware, like china,
  Once flawed is good for naught;   95
When whole, though worth a guinea,
  When broke's not worth a groat.

[2]

A woman at St. James's,
  With guineas you obtain,
But stay till lost her fame is,   100
  She'll be cheap in Drury Lane.   [*Exit.*]

[I.xii]   Sweetissa *and* Margery.

SWEETISSA.

Ungrateful, barbarous wretch!

MARGERY.

What is the matter?

SWEETISSA.

Oh Margery! Robin—

MARGERY.

What, more of him?

SWEETISSA.

Oh, worse than you can imagine—worse than I could have   5
dreaded. Oh, he has sullied my virtue!

MARGERY.

How, your virtue?

SWEETISSA.

Yes, Margery, that virtue which I kept locked up as in a

101. S.D. *Exit*] *not in WO, GGSO,*
GSO.

cupboard; that very virtue he has abused—he has barbarously insinuated to be no virtue at all. Oh, I could have 10
borne any fate but this. I that would have carried a knapsack
through the world, so that my virtue had been safe within
it—I that would have rather been the poorest man's wife,
than the richest man's whore—to be called the miss of a
footman, that would not be the miss of a king. 15

MARGERY.

It is a melancholy thing, indeed.

SWEETISSA.

Oh Margery, men do not sufficiently understand the value
of virtue. Even footmen learn to go a-whoring of their
masters, and virtue will shortly be of no use but to stop
bottles. 20

AIR XX, *Tweedside*

What woman her virtue would keep,
　　When naught by her virtue she gains?
While she lulls her soft passions asleep,
　　She's thought but a fool for her pains:
Since valets, who learn their lords' wit, 25
　　Our virtue a bauble can call,
Why should we our ladies' steps quit,
　　Or have any virtue at all? [*Exeunt.*]

28. S.D. *Exeunt.*] *not in WO, GGSO,
GSO.*

ACT II

Scene, The Fields.
                        Mr. Apshones *and* Molly.

MR. APSHONES.

I tell you, daughter, I am doubtful whether his designs be
honorable; there is no trust in these flutt'ring fellows; they
place as much glory in winning a poor girl as a soldier does
in conquering a town. Nay, their very parents often en-
courage them in it; and when they have brought up a boy   5
to flatter and deceive the women, they think they have
given him a good education, and call him a fine gentleman.

MOLLY.

Do not, dear sir, suspect my Owen; he is made of a gentler
nature.

MR. APSHONES.

And yet I have heard that that gentle gentleman, when he   10
was at London, rummaged all the playhouses for mistresses.
Nay, you yourself have heard of his pranks in the parish; did
he not seduce the fiddler's daughter?

MOLLY.

That was the fiddler's fault; you know he sold his daughter,
and gave a receipt for the money.   15

MR. APSHONES.

Hath he not made mischief between several men and their
wives; and do you not know that he lusts after every woman
he sees, though the poor wretch does not look as if he was
quite come from nurse yet.

MOLLY.

Sure angels cannot have more sweetness in their looks than   20
he.

MR. APSHONES.

Angels! Baboons—these are the creatures that resemble our
beaux the most. If they have any sweetness in them, 'tis
from the same reason that an orange hath. Why have our

---

15. *receipt for the money*] In 1730, Prince Frederick paid £1,500 to a
hautboy player named La Tour for the services of his daughter (Egmont,
I, 92).

women fresher complexions and more health in their   25
countenances here than in London, but because we have
fewer beaux among us; in that I will have you think no
more of him, for I have no design upon him, and I will
prevent his designs upon you. If he comes here anymore, I
will acquaint his mother.   30

MOLLY.

Be first assured that his designs are not honorable, before
you rashly ruin them.

MR. APSHONES.

I will consent to no clandestine affair. Let the great rob
one another, and us if they please; I will show them the poor
can be honest. I desire only to preserve my daughter; let   35
them preserve their son.

MOLLY.

Oh, sir, would you preserve your daughter, you must
preserve her love.

AIR XXI

So deep within your Molly's heart,
  Her Owen's image lies,   40
That if with Owen she must part,
  Your wretched daughter dies.

Thus when unto the soldier's breast
  The arrow flies too sure,
When thence its fatal point you wrest,   45
  Death is his only cure.

MR. APSHONES.

Pugh, pugh, you must cure one love by another; I have a
new sweetheart for you. And I'll throw you in a new suit of
clothes into the bargain—which I can tell you is enough to
balance the affections of women of much higher rank than   50
yourself.

MOLLY.

Nothing can recompense the loss of my Owen; and as to
what he loses by me, my behavior shall make him amends.

38.1. *Air XXI*] tune unknown.

MR. APSHONES.

Poor girl, how ignorant she is of the world; but little she
knows that no qualities can make amends for the want of   55
fortune, and that fortune makes a sufficient amends for the
want of every good quality.

MOLLY.

My dear Owen I am sure will think otherwise.

AIR XXII, *Let Ambition Fire Thy Mind*

> Happy with the man I love,
>   I'll obsequious watch his will;   60
> Hottest pleasures I shall prove,
>   While his pleasures I fulfill.

> Dames, by proudest titles known,
>   Shall desire what we possess;
> And while they'd less happy own,   65
>   Grandeur is not happiness.

MR. APSHONES.

I will hear no more. Remember what I have said, and
study to be dutiful—or you are no child of mine.

                                         [*Exit.*]

MOLLY.

Oh, unhappy wretch that I am, I must have no husband,
or no father. What shall I do—or whither shall I turn? Love   70
pleads strong for a husband, duty for a father. Yes, and
duty for a husband too. But then what is one who is already
so? Well then, I will antedate my duty. I will think him my
husband before he is so. But should he then prove false, and
when I've lost my father, should I lose my husband too—   75
That is impossible; falsehood and he are incompatible.

AIR XXIII, *Sweet Are the Charms*

> Beauties shall quit their darling town,
>   Lovers shall leave the fragrant shades,
> Doctors upon the fee shall frown,
>   Parsons shall hate the masquerades;   80

---

68. S.D. *Exit*] *not in WO, GGSO,
GSO.*

Nay, ere I think of Owen ill,
Women shall leave their dear quadrille.

[II.ii]   *The Field.*
Owen, Molly.

OWEN.

My dear Molly, let not the reflection on my past gaieties
give thee any uneasiness; be assured I have long been tired
with variety, and I find after all the changes I have run
through both of women and clothes—a man hath need of
no more than one woman, and one suit at a time.   5

AIR XXIV, *Under the Greenwood Tree*

To wanton pleasures, roving charms,
    I bid a long adieu,
While wrapped within my Molly's arms,
    I find enough in you.
By houses this, by horses that,   10
    By clothes a third's undone,
While this abides, the second rides,
    The third can wear but one.

MOLLY.

My dear, I will believe thee, and am resolved from this day
forward to run all the hazards of my life with thee. Let thy   15
rich parents, or my poor parents, say what they will; let us
henceforth have no other desire than to make one another
parents.

OWEN.

With all my heart, my dear; and the sooner we begin to love,
the sooner we shall be so.   20

MOLLY.

Begin to love— Alas, my dear, is it now to begin?

OWEN.

Not the theory of love, my angel. To that I have long been
an apprentice, so long that I now desire to set up my trade.

0.1. *The Field.*] *GGSO; not in GSO.*

MOLLY.

Let us then to the parson. I am as willing to be married as
thou art.   25

OWEN.

Why the parson, my dear?

MOLLY.

We can't be married without him.

OWEN.

No, but we can love without him; and what have we to do
with marriage while we can love? Marriage is but a dirty
road to love, and those are happiest who arrive at love   30
without traveling through it.

AIR XXV, *Dimi Caro*

Dearest charmer
Will you still bid me tell,
What you discern so well
By my expiring sighs;   35
My doting eyes?
Look through the instructive grove,
Each object prompts to love,
Hear how the turtles coo,
All nature tells you what to do.   40

MOLLY.

Too well I understand you now. No, no, however dirty the
road of marriage be, I will to love no other way. Alas!
There is no other way but one, and that is dirtier still. None
travel through it without sullying their reputations beyond
the possibility of cleaning.   45

OWEN.

When cleanliness is out of fashion, who would desire to be
clean? And when ladies of quality appear with dirty
reputations, why should you fear a little spot on yours?

MOLLY.

Ladies of quality may wear bad reputations as well as bad
clothes, and be admired in both. But women of lower rank   50
must be decent, or they will be disregarded; for no woman

31.1. *Dimi Caro*] *GGSO; Dearest*
charmer GSO.

can pass without one good quality, unless she be a woman
of very great quality.

OWEN.

You judge too severely. Nature never prompts us to a real
crime. It is the imposition of a priest, not nature's voice,   55
which bars us from a pleasure allowed to every beast but
man. But why do I this to convince thee by arguments of
what thou art sufficiently certain? Why should I refute your
tongue, when your fond eyes refute it?

AIR XXVI, *Canny Boatman*

How can I trust your words precise,   60
My soft desires denying,
When, oh! I read within your eyes,
Your tender heart complying.
    Your tongue may cheat,
    And with deceit   65
Your softer wishes cover;
    But, oh! your eyes
    Know no disguise,
Nor ever cheat your lover.

MOLLY.

Away, false perjured barbarous wretch. Is this the love you   70
have for me to undo me, to ruin me?

OWEN.

Oh, do not take on thee thus, my dear Molly. I would
sooner ruin myself than thee.

MOLLY.

Ay, so it appears. Oh, fool that I was to think thou could'st
be constant who hast ruined so many women. To think that   75
thou ever didst intend to marry me, who hast long been
practised in the arts of seducing our sex. Henceforth I will
sooner think it possible for butter to come when the witch
is in the churn, for hay to dry in the rain, for wheat to be

54–55. *Nature . . . crime*] perhaps a reference to the Shaftesburian idea of
innate natural goodness. As Fielding uses the idea here, it is clearly meant
to be seen as fallacious.

78–79. *witch . . . churn*] a reference to a superstition that an evil spirit
was present when butter did not form in a churn (Edwin and Mona A.
Radford, *Encyclopaedia of Superstitions* [New York, 1949], p. 54).

ripe at Christmas, for cheese to be made without milk, for a   80
barn to be free from mice, for a warren to be free from rats,
for a cherry orchard to be free from blackbirds, or for a
churchyard to be free from ghosts, as for a young man to be
free from falsehood.

OWEN.

Be not enraged, my sweetest dear; let me kiss away thy   85
passion.

MOLLY.

Avaunt! A blight is in thy kiss—thy breath is the wind of
wantonness—and virtue cannot grow near thee.

AIR XXVII, *I'll Range Around*

Since you so base and faithless be,
And would— without marrying me,   90
A maid I'll go to Pluto's shore,
Nor think of men or—marriage more.   [*Exit.*]

OWEN.

You'll repent that resolution before you get half way—
She'll go pout and pine away half an hour by herself, then
relapse into a fit of fondness, and be all my own.   95

AIR XXVIII, *Cloe Is False*

Women in vain love's powerful torrent
   With unequal strength oppose,
Reason a while may stem the strong current,
   Love still at last her soul o'erflows;
      Pleasures inviting,   100
      Passions exciting,
      Her lover charms her,
      Of pride disarms her,
      Down she goes.   [*Exit.*]

[II.iii]   *A Field.*
              Robin, William, John, Thomas.

WILL.

Here's as proper a place as can be for our business.

92. S.D. *Exit*] *not in WO; GGSO,*   104. S.D. *Exit*] *not in WO, GGSO,*
GSO.   *GSO.*

ROBIN.

The sooner the better.

JOHN.

Come, Thomas, thou and I will not be idle.

THOMAS.

I'll take a knock or two for love with all my heart.

[*They strip.*]

AIR XXIX, *Britons Strike Home*

WILL.	Robin, come on, come on, come on,	5
	As soon as you please.	
ROBIN.	Will, I will hit thee a slap in the,	
	Slap in the, slap in the face.	
WILL.	Would, would I could see it,	
	I would with both feet,	10
	Give thee such a kick by the by.	
ROBIN.	If you dare, sir, do.	
WILL.	Why do not, sir, you.	
ROBIN.	I'm ready, I'm ready.	
WILL.	And so am I too.	15

THOMAS.

You must fight to some other tune, or you will never fight at all.

[II.iv]   Robin, Will, John, Thomas, Susan.

SUSAN.

What are you doing? You set of lazy rascals, do you consider my master will be at home within these two hours, and find nothing ready for his supper?

WILL.

Let Master come when he will. If he keeps Robin, I am free to go as soon as he pleases; Robin and I will not live in one   5
house together.

SUSAN.

Why, what's the matter?

[II.iii]   *in GGSO, GSO.*
4. S.D. *They strip.*] *stript WO; not*
_____

[II.iii]
5–15.] This song is a burlesque of the famous duel between Pulteney and Lord Hervey in January, 1731.

ROBIN.

He wanted to get my mistress from me, that's all.

WILL.

You lie, sirrah, you lie.

ROBIN.

Who do you call liar? You blockhead, I say you lie.   10

WILL.

And I say you lie.

ROBIN.

And you lie.

WILL.

And I say you lie again.

ROBIN.

The devil take the greatest liar, I say.

AIR XXX, *Mother, Quoth Hodge*

SUSAN.   Oh fie upon't, Robin; oh fie upon't, Will.   15
   What language like this, what scullion defames?
  'Twere better your tongues should ever be still,
   Than always be scolding and calling vile names.

WILL.   'Twas he that lies
    Did first devise.   20
  The first words were his, and the last shall be mine.

ROBIN.   You kiss my dog.

WILL.   You're a sly dog.

ROBIN.   Loggerhead.

WILL.   Blockhead.   25

ROBIN.   Fool.

WILL.   Fox.

ROBIN.   Swine.

WILL.

Sarrah, I'll make you repent you ever quarreled with me.
I will tell my master of two silver spoons you stole. I'll   30
discover your tricks: your selling of glasses and pretending
the frost broke them; making master brew more beer than
he needed, and then giving it away to your own family,
especially to feed the great swollen belly of that fat-gutted

---

34–35. *fat-gutted brother*] a reference to Sir Robert Walpole's younger
brother Horatio, who had been granted public office. This Horatio is sometimes called "Old Horace" to distinguish him from his more famous nephew.

brother of yours, who gets drunk twice a day at Master's   35
expense.

ROBIN.

Ha, ha, ha! And is this all?

WILL.

No, sarrah, it is not all. Then there's your filing the plate,
and when it was found lighter, pretending that it wasted in
cleaning; and your bills for tutty and rotten-stone, when   40
you used nothing but poor whiting. Sarrah, you have been
such a rogue, that you have stole above half my master's
plate, and spoiled the rest.

SUSAN.

Fie upon't, William, what have we to do with Master's
losses? He is rich and can afford it. Don't let us quarrel   45
among ourselves. Let us stand by one another, for let me tell
you, if matters were to be too nicely examined into, I am
afraid it would go hard with us all. Wise servants always
stick close to one another, like plums in a pudding that's
over-wetted—says Susan the cook.   50

JOHN.

Or horse in a stable that's on fire—says John the groom.

THOMAS.

Or grapes upon a wall—says Thomas the gardener.

SUSAN.

Every servant should be sauce to his fellow servant. As
sauce disguises the faults of a dish, so should he theirs. Oh
William, were we all to have our deserts, we should be   55
finely roasted indeed.

AIR XXXI, *Dame of Honor*

A wise man others' faults conceals,
  His own to get more clear of;
While folly all she knows reveals,
  Sure what she does to hear of.   60
The parson and the lawyer's blind,
  Each to his brother's erring—
For should you search, he knows you'd find
  No barrel the better herring.

40, 41. *tutty, rotten-stone, whiting*] substances used in polishing.

AIR XXXII, *We've Cheated the Parson*

ROBIN. Here stands honest Bob, who ne'er in his life   65
      Was known to be guilty of faction and strife.
           But oh what can
           Appease the man,
      Who'd rob me of both my place and my wife.
WILL. If you prove it, I will be hanged, and that's fair,   70
ROBIN. I've that in my pocket will make it appear,
WILL.   Prithee what?
ROBIN.   Ask you that,
      When you know you have written against me so flat?
ROBIN [*showing* Will *the letter*].

Here is your hand, though there is not your name to it. Is   75
not this your hand, sir?

WILL.

I don't think it worth my while to tell you whether it is or no.

ROBIN.

Was it not enough to try to supplant me in my place, but
you must try to get my mistress?

WILL.

Your mistress! Any man may have your mistress that can   80
outbid you; for it is very well known, you never had a
mistress without paying for her.

ROBIN.

But perhaps you may find me too cunning for you, and
while you are attempting my place, you may lose your own.

AIR XXXIII, *Hark, Hark, the Cock Crows*

WILL.   When Master thinks fit,   85
      I am ready to quit
         A place I so little regard, sir;
      For while thou art here,
      No merit must e'er
         Expect to find any reward, sir.   90
      The groom that is able
      To manage his stable
         Of places enough need not doubt, sir;

75. S.D. *showing . . . letter*] *not in*
WO, GGSO, GSO.

> But you, my good brother,
> Will scarce find another,   95
> If Master should e'er turn you out, sir.

SUSAN.

If you can't be friends without it, you had best fight it out
once for all.

WILL.

Ay, so say I.

ROBIN.

No, no, I am for no fighting. It is but a word and a blow 100
with William; he would set the whole parish together by
the ears, if he could; and it is very well known what
difficulties I have been put to, to keep peace in it.

WILL.

I suppose peacemaking is one of the secret services you have
done Master, for they are such secrets, that your friend the 105
devil can hardly discover. And whence does your peacemaking arise but from your fears of getting a black eye or
bloody nose in the squabble? For if you could set the whole
parish a-boxing, without boxing yourself, it is well known
you would do it, sarrah, sarrah. Had your love for the 110
tenants been the occasion of your peacemaking, as you call
it, you would not be always making Master so hard upon
them in every court, and prevent him giving them the fat
ox at Christmas, on pretense of good husbandry.

ROBIN.

Yours you have a great love for, master; we know by your 115
driving to inch, as you do, sirrah. You are such a headstrong
devil that you will overturn the coach one day or other, and
break both Master and Mistress' necks. It is always neck or
nothing with you.

SUSAN.

Oh fie! William, pray let me be the mediator between you. 120

ROBIN.

Ay, ay, let Susan be the mediator. I'll refer my cause to
anyone; it is equal to me.

105. Master] *GGSO;* masters *GSO.*

106–7. *peacemaking*] a reference to Walpole's policy of keeping the nation
at peace when some of his opponents urged him to be bellicose.

116. *to inch*] apparently an understatement meaning "recklessly, care-
lessly, within an inch of ruin."

WILL.

No, no, I shall not refer an affair, wherein my honor is so
concerned, to a woman.

AIR XXXIV, *Of a Noble Race Was Shinken*

Good Madam Cook, the greasy,   125
Pray leave your saucy bawling,
    Let all your toil
    Be to make the pot boil,
For that's your proper calling.

With men as wise as Robin,   130
A female judge may pass, sir;
    For where the grey mare
    Is the better horse, there
The horse is but an ass, sir.

        [*Exeunt* Will *and* John.]

[II.v]   Robin, Thomas, Susan.

SUSAN.

Saucy fellow.

THOMAS.

I suppose he is gone to inform Master against you.

ROBIN.

Let him go. I am too well with Madam to fear any mischief
he can make with Master. And heark'ee, between you and
I, Madam won't suffer me to be turned out. You heard   5
William upbraid me with stealing the beer for my own
family; but she knows half of it hath gone to her own private
cellar, where she and the parson sit and drink, and meditate
way to propagate religion in the parish.

SUSAN.

Don't speak against Madam, Robin; she is an exceeding   10
good woman to her own servants.

ROBIN.

Ay, ay, to us upper servants. We that keep the keys fare well
enough; and for the rest, let them starve for Robin. It's the
way of the world, Susan; the heads of all professions thrive,
while the others starve.   15

134.1. *Exeunt* Will *and* John.] *Exit.*
GGSO; not in GSO.

AIR XXXV, *Pierot's Tune*

Great courtiers palaces contain,
    While small ones fear the jail,
Great parsons riot in champagne,
    Small parsons sot on ale;
Great whores in coaches gang,   20
        Smaller misses,
        For their kisses,
    Are in Bridewell banged;
        While in vogue
        Lives the great rogue,   25
Small rogues are by dozens hanged.

                    [*Exit with* Thomas.]

[II.vi]   Susan, Sweetissa.

SWEETISSA.
Oh brave Susan! What, you are resolved to keep open
doings? When a woman goes without the precincts of
virtue, she never knows where to stop.

AIR XXXVI, *Country Garden*

Virtue within a woman's heart,
    By nature's hand is rammed in,   5
There must be kept by steady art,
    Like water when it's dammed in.
        But the dam once broken,
        Past all revoking,
    Virtue flies off in a minute;   10
        Like a river left,
        Of waters bereft,
    Each man may venture in it.

SUSAN.
I hope you will pardon my want of capacity, madam, but I
don't know what you mean.   15

SWEETISSA.
Your capacity is too capacious, madam.

26.1. *Exit with* Thomas.] *GGSO;*
not in GSO.

SUSAN.

Your method of talking, madam, is something dark.

SWEETISSA.

Your method of acting is darker, madam.

SUSAN.

I dare appeal to the whole world for the justification of my
actions, madam; and I defy anyone to say my fame is more   20
sullied than my plates, madam.

SWEETISSA.

Your pots you mean, madam. If you are like any plates, it
is soup plates, which any man may put his spoon into.

SUSAN.

Me, madam?

SWEETISSA.

You, madam.   25

AIR XXXVII, *Dainty Davy*

SUSAN.   What the devil mean you thus
                    Scandal scattering,
                    Me bespattering,
                Dirty slut, and ugly puss,
                    What can be your meaning?   30
SWEETISSA.   Had you, madam, not forgot,
                When with Bob you—you know what,
                    Surely, madam, you would not
                    Twice inquire my meaning.

There, read that letter, and be satisfied how base you have   35
been to a woman to whom you have professed a friendship.

SUSAN.

What do you mean by offering me a letter to read, when
you know—

SWEETISSA.

When I know you writ it, madam.

SUSAN.

When you know I can neither write nor read, madam. It   40
was my parents' fault, not mine, that gave me not a better
education; and if you had not been taught to write, you
would have been no more able to write than myself—though
you barbarously upbraid me with what is not my fault.

–43–

SWEETISSA.

How! And is it possible you can neither read nor write? 45

SUSAN.

Possible! Why should it be impossible for a servant not to be able to write, when so many gentlemen can't spell?

SWEETISSA.

Here is your name to a love letter which is directed to Robin, wherein you complain of his having left you after he had enjoyed you. 50

SUSAN.

Enjoyed me?

SWEETISSA.

It is so, I assure you.

SUSAN.

If ever I had anything to say to Robin, but as one fellow servant might say to another fellow servant, may my pot ne'er boil again. 55

SWEETISSA.

I am sorry you cannot read, that you might see the truth of what I say, that you might read *Susan Roastmeat* in plain letters. And if you did not write it yourself, sure the devil must have writ it for you.

SUSAN.

I think I have said enough to satisfy you, and as much as is 60 consistent with my honor.

SWEETISSA.

You have, indeed, to satisfy me of your innocence. Nor do I think it inconsistent with my honor to assure you I am sorry I said what I said. I do, and humbly ask your pardon, madam. 65

SUSAN.

Dear madam, this acknowledgement from you is sufficient. Oh Sweetissa, had I been one of those, I might have had to do with my young master.

SWEETISSA.

Nay, for that matter, we might all have had to do with my young master; that argues little in your defense. But this I 70

62. your] *GGSO;* you *GSO.*

am assured of: if you cannot write at all you did not write
the letter.

AIR XXXVIII, *Valentine's Day*

A woman must her honor save,
While she's a virgin found;
And he can hardly be a knave,   75
Who is not worth a pound.
On horseback he who cannot ride,
On horseback did not rob;
And since a pen you cannot guide,
You never wrote to Bob.   *Exeunt.* 80

[II.vii]   Owen *and* Mr. Apshones.

MR. APSHONES.

I desire not, Mr. Owen, that you would marry my daughter.
I had rather see her married to one of her own degree. I had
rather have a set of fine healthy grandchildren ask me
blessing, than a poor puny breed of half-begotten brats, that
inherit the diseases as well as the titles of their parents.   5

OWEN.

Pshaw, pshaw, Master Apshones, these are the narrow
sentiments of such old fellows as you that have either never
known or forgotten the world, that think their daughters
going out of the world if they go five miles from them, and
had rather see them walk a foot at home than ride in a   10
coach abroad.

MR. APSHONES.

I would not see her ride in her coach this year, to see her
ride in an hearse the next.

OWEN.

You may never arrive to that honor, good sir.

MR. APSHONES.

I would not advise you to attempt bringing any dishonor   15
on us. That may not be so safe as you imagine.

OWEN.

So safe?

80. S.D. *Exeunt*] *GGSO; not in*
GSO.

MR. APSHONES.

No, not so safe, sir. I have not lost my spirit with my fortune;
I am your father's tenant, but not his slave. Though you
have ruined many poor girls with impunity, you may not   20
always succeed so; for, let me tell you, sir, whoever brings
dishonor on me shall bring ruin on himself.

OWEN.

Ha, ha, ha.

MR. APSHONES.

I believe both Sir Owen and her ladyship too good people to
suffer you in these practices, were they acquainted with   25
them. Sir Owen hath still behaved as the best of landlords.
He knows a landlord should protect, not prey on his
tenants—should be the shepherd, not the wolf to his flock.
But one would have thought you imagined we lived under
that barbarous custom I have read of when the landlord was   30
intitled to the maidenheads of all his tenants' daughters.

OWEN.

Ha, ha, ha! Thou art a very ridiculous, comical, odd sort
of an old fellow, faith.

MR. APSHONES.

It is very likely you and I may appear in the same light to
one another. Your dress would have made as ridiculous a   35
figure in my young days as mine does now. What is the
meaning of all that plaistering upon your wig, unless you
would insinuate that your brains lie on the outside of your
heads?

OWEN.

Your daughter likes our dress, if you don't.   40

MR. APSHONES.

I desire you would spare my daughter, sir. I shall take as
much care of her as I can. And if you should prevail on her
to her ruin, be assured your father's estate should not
secure you from my revenge. You should find that the true
spirit of English liberty acknowledges no superior equal to   45
oppression.   [*Exit.*]

OWEN.

The true spirit of English liberty—ha, ha, ha! Thou art not

46. S.D. *Exit*] *not in GGSO, GSO.*

the first father, or husband, that hath blustered in this
manner, and been afterwards as quiet as a lamb. He were a
fine gallant, indeed, who would be stopped in the pursuit of   50
his mistress by the threatenings of her relations. Not that I
should care to venture, if I thought the fellow in earnest,
but your heroes in words are never so in deeds.

AIR XXXIX, *My Cloe, Why Do You Slight Me*

The whore of fame is jealous,
  The coward would seem brave;   55
For we are still most zealous,
  What most we want to have.
    The madman boasts his senses,
    And he whose chief pretense is
    To liberty's defense, is   60
  Too oft the greatest slave.

[II.viii]   Owen *and* Molly.

OWEN.
  She here!
MOLLY.
  Cruel, dost thou fly me? Am I become hateful in thy sight?
  Are all thy wicked vows forgotten? For sure if thou didst
  even remember them, they would oblige thee to another
  behavior.   5
OWEN.
  Can you blame me for obeying your commands in shunning
  you? Sure you have forgotten your last vows, never to see
  me more.
MOLLY.
  Alas, you know too well that I am as insincere in every
  repulse to you as you have been in your advances to me.   10
  How unjustly do men accuse us of using a lover ill, when
  we are no sooner in his power than he uses us so?

AIR XL, *Sylvia My Dearest*

Cruelest creature, why have you wooed me,
Why thus pursued me
Into love's snare?   15

—47—

> While I was cruel,
> I was your jewel;
> Now I am kind, you bid me despair.
>
> Nature's sweet flowers
>   Warm seasons nourish,   20
> In summer flourish,
>   Winter's their bane:
> Love against nature
>   Checked, grows the greater,
> And best is nourished with cold disdain.   25

OWEN.

How canst thou wrong me so, my dear Molly? Your father
hath been here, and insulted me in the rudest manner; but
notwithstanding that, I am resolved—

MOLLY.

To fulfill your promise, and marry me.

OWEN.

Why dost thou mention that hateful word? That, that is the   30
cruel frost which nips the flower of love. Politeness is not a
greater enemy to honesty, nor quadrille to common sense,
than marriage is to love. They are fire and water, and
cannot live together. Marriage is the only thing thou
shouldst ask that I would not grant.   35

MOLLY.

And till you grant that, I will grant nothing else.

OWEN.

It is for your sake I would not marry you, for I could never
love if I was confined to it.

AIR XLI

> How happy's the swain,
> Whom beauty firing,   40
> All admiring,
> All desiring,
> Never desiring in vain.
> How happy to rove,
> Through sweetest bowers,   45

38.1. *Air XLI*] tune unknown.

And cull the flowers,
In the delicious garden of love.
How wretched the soul,
Under control,
To one poor choice confined a while,   50
   Wanton it exerts the lass,
No, no, let the joys of my life,
   Like the years in circles roll.
But since you are so ungrateful,
Since my service is so hateful,   55
   Willing I my place forsake.   [*Exit.*]

MOLLY.

He's gone! He's lost forever, irrevocably lost! Oh virtue,
where's thy force? Where are those thousand charms that
we are told lie in thee, when lovers cannot see them?
Should Owen e'er return, should he renew his entreaties, I   60
fear his success; for I find every day love attains more and
more ground of virtue.

AIR XLII, *Midsummer Wish*

When love is lodged within the heart,
Poor virtue to the outworks flies,
   The tongue in thunder takes its part,   65
And darts in lightning from the eyes.

From lips and eyes with gested grace,
In vain she keeps out charming him,
   For love will find some weaker place,
To let the dear invader in.   [*Exit.*]   70

56. S.D. *Exit*] *not in GGSO, GSO.*   70. S.D. *Exit*] *not in GGSO, GSO.*

ACT III

Scene, Sir Owen Apshinken's House
                        Sir Owen, *smoking.*

SIR OWEN.

What a glorious creature was he who first discovered the
use of tobacco. The industrious retires from business, the
voluptuous from pleasure, the lover from a cruel mistress,
the husband from a cursed wife, and I from all the world
to my pipe.   5

AIR XLIII, *Free Mason's Tune*

Let the learned talk of books,
    The glutton of cooks,
The lover of Celia's soft smack-o;
    No mortal can boast
    So noble a toast,   10
As a pipe of accepted tobacco.

Let the soldier for fame,
    And a gen'ral's name,
In battle get many a thwack-o;
    Let who will have most,   15
    Who will rule the roast,
Give me but a pipe of tobacco.

Tobacco gives wit
    To the dullest old cit,
And makes him of politics crack-o;   20
    The lawyers i'th' hall,
    Were not able to bawl,
Were it not for a whiff of tobacco.

The man whose chief glory
    Is telling of story,   25
Had never arrived at the knack-o,
    Between ev'ry haying,
    And as I was saying,
Did he not take a whiff of tobacco.

The doctor who places   30
Much skill in grimaces,
And feels your pulse running tick-tack-o;
    Would you know his chief skill?
    It is only to fill,
And smoke a good pipe of tobacco.   35

The courtiers alone
To this weed are not prone;
Would you know what 'tis makes them so slack-o?
    'Twas because it inclined
    To be honest the mind,   40
And therefore they banished tobacco.

[III.ii]   Sir Owen *and* Lady Apshinken.

LADY APSHINKEN.

It is very hard, my dear, that I must be an eternal slave to
my family; that the moment my back is turned, everything
goes to rack and manger; that you will take no care upon
yourself, like a sleepy good-for-nothing drone as you are.

SIR OWEN.

My wife is a very good wife, only a little inclined to talking.   5
If she had no tongue, or I had no ears, we should be the
happiest couple in Wales.

LADY APSHINKEN.

Sir Owen, Sir Owen, it is very well known what offers I
refused when I married you.

SIR OWEN.

Yes, my dear, it is very well known, indeed; I have heard   10
of it often enough, in conscience. But this I am confident: if
you had ever had a better offer, you knew your own interest
too well to have refused it.

LADY APSHINKEN.

Ungrateful man! If I have shown that I know the value of
money, it has been for your interest as well as mine. And let   15
me tell you, sir, whenever my conscience hath struggled with
my interest, she hath always got the better.

8–9. *what . . . refused*] Before her marriage to George II, Queen Caroline
had refused an offer of marriage from the Catholic Archduke Charles of
Austria, who later became the emperor (Lucas, p. 7).

SIR OWEN.

Why possibly it may be so, for I am sure whichever side
your tongue is of will get the better. And hark ye, my dear,
I fancy your conscience and your tongue lie very near   20
together. As for your interest, it lies too near your heart to
have any intercourse with your tongue.

LADY APSHINKEN.

Methinks, Sir Owen, you should be the last who reflected on
me for scolding your servants.

SIR OWEN.

So I would, if you would not scold at me. Vent your ill   25
nature on all the parish, let me and my tobacco alone, and
I care not: but a scolding wife to me is a walking bass viol
out of tune.

LADY APSHINKEN.

Sir, sir, a drunken husband is a bad fiddlestick to that bass
viol, never able to put her into tune, nor to play any tune   30
upon her.

SIR OWEN.

A scolding wife is rosin to that fiddlestick, continually
rubbing it up to play, till it wear out.

AIR XLIV, *Tenant of My Own*

Of all bad sorts of wives
   The scolds are sure the worst,   35
With a hum, drum, scum, hurry scurry scum.
   Would I'd a cuckold been,
   Ere I had been accursed
With your hum, drum, [scum, hurry scurry scum.]

   Would he have cursed mankind   40
   (If Juno's drawn to life)
When Jupiter Pandora sent,
   He should have sent his wife,
With her hum, drum, [scum, hurry scurry scum,
With her hum, drum, scum, hurry scurry scum.]   45
                     [*Exit.*]

39. drum . . . scum.] drum, etc.   44–45. drum, . . . scurry   scum.]
GGSO, GSO.   drum, etc. *GGSO, GSO.*
                               45.1. *Exit*] *not in GGSO, GSO.*

[III.iii]   Lady Apshinken *and* Susan.

LADY APSHINKEN.

Go thy ways, for an errant knight as thou art. —So, Susan,
what bring you?

SUSAN.

The bill of fare, madam.

LADY APSHINKEN.

The bill of fare! This looks more like a bill for a month than
a day.   5

SUSAN.

Master hath invited several of the tenants today, madam.

LADY APSHINKEN.

Yes, I am acquainted with your master's generosity. He
would keep a tenant's table by his consent. On my conscience, he would suffer some of the poorer tenants to eat
more than their rent out.   10

SUSAN.

Heaven bless him for such goodness!

LADY APSHINKEN.

This sirloin of beef may stand, only cut off half of it for
tomorrow. It is too big for one dish.

SUSAN.

Oh dear madam, it is a thousand pities to cut it.

LADY APSHINKEN.

Pshaw! I tell you no polite people suffer a large dish to come   15
to their table. I have seen an entertainment of three courses
where the substance of the whole would not have made half
a sirloin of beef.

SUSAN.

The devil take such politeness, I say.

LADY APSHINKEN [*reading the bill of fare and commenting on it*].

"A goose roasted." —Very well, take a particular care of the   20
giblets; they bear a very good price in the market. "Two
brace of partridges." —I'll leave out one of them. "An apple
pie, with quinces." —Why quinces, when you know quinces
are so dear? —There; and for the rest, do you keep it, and
let me have two dishes a day till it is out.   25

19.1. S.D. *Reading ... it.*] *not   in*
GGSO, GSO.

—53—

SUSAN.

Why, madam, half the provision will stink at that rate.

LADY APSHINKEN.

Then they will eat the less of it. I know some good house-
wives that never buy any other, for it is always cheap, and
will go the farther.

SUSAN.

So, as the smell of the old English hospitality used to invite   30
people in, that of the present is to keep them away.

LADY APSHINKEN.

Old English hospitality! Oh, don't name it; I am sick at
the sound.

SUSAN.

Would I had lived in those days! I wish I had been born a
cook in an age when there was some business for one, before   35
we had learnt this French politeness and been taught to
dress our meat by nations that have no meat to dress.

AIR XLV, *The King's Old Courtier*

When mighty roast beef was the Englishman's food,
It ennobled our hearts, and enriched our blood,
Our soldiers were brave, and our courtiers were good.   40
    Oh the roast beef of England,
    And old England's roast beef!

But since we have learnt from all-conquering France,
To eat their ragouts as well as to dance,
Oh what a fine figure we make in romance!   45
    Oh the roast beef of England,
    And old England's roast beef!   [*Exit.*]

LADY APSHINKEN.

Servants are continually jealous of the least thrift of a
master or mistress; they are never easy but when they
observe extravagance.   50

47. S.D. *Exit*] *not in GGSO, GSO.*

[III.iv]   Lady Apshinken *and* Puzzletext.

AIR XLVI, *Oh Jenny, Oh Jenny*

LADY APSHINKEN.   Oh Doctor, oh Doctor, where hast thou been?
                  Sure woman was never like me perplexed!
                  I have been chiding:
PUZZLETEXT.   I have been riding,
                  And meditating upon my text.   5

LADY APSHINKEN.

I wish you would give us a sermon on charity, that my
servants might know that it is no charity to indulge a
voluptuous appetite.

PUZZLETEXT.

There is, madam, as your ladyship very well knows, a
religious charity, and an irreligious charity. Now the   10
religious charity teaches us rather to starve the belly of our
friend, than feed it. Verily, starving is voluptuous food for a
sinful constitution.

LADY APSHINKEN.

I wish, Doctor, when you go next to London, you would buy
me up, at the cheapest rates, all the books on charity that   15
have been published.

PUZZLETEXT.

I have a treatise, madam, which I shall shortly publish, that
will comprehend the whole. It will be writ in Latin, and
dedicated to your ladyship.

LADY APSHINKEN.

Anything for the encouragement of religion. I am a great   20
admirer of the Latin language. I believe, Doctor, I now
understand Latin as well as English. —But oh, Doctor, it
gives me pain, very great pain, that notwithstanding all our
endeavours, there should yet remain so many wicked people
in our parish. One of the tenants, the other day, abused his   25
wife in the most terrible manner. Shall I never make them
use their wives tolerably?

AIR XLVII

LADY APSHINKEN.   Ah, Doctor, I long much as misers for pelf,
                  To see the whole parish as good as myself.

27.1. *Air XLVII*] tune unknown.

PUZZLETEXT.   Ah, madam, your ladyship need not to
                        doubt,   30
                     But that by my sermons will be soon brought
                        about.

LADY APSHINKEN.   Ah, man, can your sermons put 'em in the
                        right way,
                     When not one in ten e'er hears what you
                        say?

PUZZLETEXT   Ah, madam, your ladyship need not to fear;
                     If you make them pay, but I'll make them
                        hear.   35

[III.v]   *To them*, Robin.

                     AIR XLVIII, *In Porus*

ROBIN.   Some confounded planet reigning,
                     Surely hath, beyond explaining,
                          Your sex beguiled,
                          Sense defiled,
                          Sense awry led   5
                             To mistake:
                          I should wonder,
                          Could you blunder
                             Thus awake.
                     But if your almighty wit   10
                     Me for William will quit,
                          E'en brew as you bake.

LADY APSHINKEN.
What's the meaning of this?

ROBIN.
Is your ladyship a stranger to it then? Madam, don't you
know that I am to be turned away, and William made   15
butler?

LADY APSHINKEN.
How?

ROBIN.
Nay, I assure your ladyship it is true. I just now received a
message from Master, to give an account of the plate. And
perhaps I shall give a better account than William would,   20
had he been butler as long as I have.

LADY APSHINKEN.

I am out of all patience; I'll to Sir Owen this moment.—I
will see whether I am a cipher in this house or no.   [*Exit.*]

PUZZLETEXT.

Hark ye, Mr. Robin, you are safe enough; her ladyship is
your friend. So go you and send me a bottle of good wine   25
into my room, for I am a very good friend of yours.   [*Exit.*]

[III.vi]   Robin, *solus.*

ROBIN.

It is not that I intend to live long in the family, but I don't
care to be turned away. I would give warning myself, and
if this storm blows over, I will. Thanks to my industry, I
have made a shift to get together a little comfortable sub-
sistence for the rest of my days. I'll purchase some little snug   5
farm in Wales, of about a hundred a year, and retire with—
Ha! With whom shall I retire, since Sweetissa's false? What
avails it to me that I can purchase an estate, when I cannot
purchase happiness?

> AIR XLIX, *Cupid, God of Pleasing Anguish*
>
> What avail large sums of treasure,   10
> But to purchase sums of pleasure,
>   But your wishes to obtain?
> Poor the wretch whole worlds possessing,
> While his dearest darling blessing
> He must sigh for still in vain.   15

[III.vii]   Robin *and* Sweetissa.

ROBIN.

Where is my wealth, when the cabinet it was locked up in is
broke open and plundered?

SWEETISSA.

He's here! Love would blow me like a whirlwind to his

23. S.D. *Exit*] *not in GGSO, GSO.*   26. S.D. *Exit*] *not in GGSO, GSO.*

[III.vi]

3. *storm blows over*] One of Walpole's guiding political principles was
quieta non movere, which implied a policy of letting public opinion quietly
"blow over" a controversial issue.

arms, did not the string of honor pull me back—honor, that
forces more lies from the mouth of a woman than gold does   5
from the mouth of a lawyer.

ROBIN.

See where she stands. The false, the perjured she. Yet
guilty as she is, she would be dearer to my soul than light,
did not my honor interpose. My honor, which cannot
suffer me to wed a whore. I must part with honor, or with   10
her; and a servant without honor is a wretch indeed. How
happy are men of quality, who cannot lose their honor, do
what they will. Right honor is tried in roguery, as gold is in
the fire, and comes out still the same.

AIR L, *Dame of Honor*

Nice honor by a private man   15
   With zeal must be maintained;
For soon 'tis lost, and never can
   By any be regained.
But once right honorable grown,
   He's then its rightful owner;   20
For though the worst of rogues he's known,
   He still is a man of honor.

SWEETISSA.

I wish I could impute this blindness of yours to love. But,
alas, love would see me, not my faults. You see my faults,
not me.   25

ROBIN.

I wish it were possible to see you faultless. But alas, you are
so hemmed in with faults, one must see through them to
come at you.

SWEETISSA.

I know of none, but loving you too well.

ROBIN.

That may be one, perhaps, if you were great with William.   30

SWEETISSA.

Oh Robin, if thou art resolved to be false, do not, I beseech
thee, do not let thy malice conspire to ruin my reputation.

ROBIN [*giving her a letter*].

There, madam, read that letter once more, then bid me be
tender of your reputation, if you can—though women have

always the boldest claims to reputation when they have the   35
least pretensions to it. For virtue, like gunpowder, never
makes any noise till it goes off: when you hear the report,
you may be sure it's gone.

SWEETISSA.

This is some conspiracy against me, for may the devil fetch
me this instant if I ever saw this letter before.   40

ROBIN.

What, and drop it from your pocket?

SWEETISSA.

Oh base man! If ever I suffered William to kiss me in my
life, unless we have been at questions and commands, may
I never—be kissed while I live again. And if I am not a
maid now, may I die as good a maid as I am now. But you   45
shall see that I am not the only one who can receive letters,
and drop them from their pockets too. [*She gives him a
letter.*]   —There, if thou art guilty, that letter will shock
thee, while innocence guards me.

AIR LI, *Why Will Florella*

When guilt within the bosom lies,   50
    A thousand ways it speaks,
It stares affrighted through the eyes,
    And blushes through the cheeks.

But innocence, disdaining fear,
    Adorns the injured face,   55
And while the black accuser's near,
    Shines forth with brighter grace.

ROBIN [*having read the letter*].

Surprising! Sure some little writing devil lurks in the house.
Ha! A thought hath just shot through my brain.—Sweetissa,
if you have virtue, if you have honor, if you have humanity,   60
answer me one question: did the parson ever make love to
you?

SWEETISSA.

Why do you ask me that?

58. S.D. *Having . . . letter.*]   *not in*
GGSO, GSO.

ROBIN [*showing both letters*].

    These two letters are writ by the same hand. And if they
were not writ by William, they must have been by the 65
parson; for no one else, I believe, can write or read in the
house.

SWEETISSA.

    I can't say he hath, nor I can't say he hath not. Once he
told me that if I was worth a hundred pound he'd marry me.

ROBIN.

    Did he? That's enough; by George I'll make an example of 70
him. I'll beat him till he has as great an aversion to marriage
as any priest in Rome hath.

SWEETISSA.

    Oh fie! What, beat the parson?

ROBIN.

    Never tell me of the parson. If he will have my meat, I'll
give him some sauce to it. 75

SWEETISSA.

    Consider, good Robin; for though thou hast been a base
man to me, I would not have thee damned.

ROBIN.

    The parson would send me to heaven, I thank him. I'd
rather be damned then go to heaven as the parson's cuckold.
'Sbud! I'll souse him till he shall have as little appetite for 80
woman's flesh as horse flesh.

AIR LII, *Hunt the Squirrel*

SWEETISSA.   Oh for goodness sake forbear!
        Think he's a parson, think he's a parson;
      Look upon the cloth he wears,
        Ere you pull his ears. 85

ROBIN.   Cease your chattering, I will batter him;
      Blood and thunderbolt!
      I'll rub him, drub him, scrub him down,
        As jockeys do a colt.   [*Exit.*]

SWEETISSA.

    He's gone; perhaps will knock the parson in the head. What 90

89. S.D. *Exit*] *not in GGSO, GSO.*

can he then expect but to be hanged by the neck? Oh, that he were hanged once safe about my neck.—Ye powers, preserve him from the hangman's noose, and tie him fast in Hymen's.

[III.viii]   Sweetissa *and* John.

SWEETISSA.

Oh John, fly! If thou wilt save thy friend, fly up into the parson's closet.

JOHN.

What's the matter?

SWEETISSA.

One moment's delay, and Robin's lost. He is gone in a mighty passion to beat the parson. Run and prevent him,   5
for if he should kill the parson, he will be hanged.

JOHN.

Kill him! If he lifts up his hand against him, he will be put into the spiritual court, and that's worse than hanging.

SWEETISSA.

Fly, fly, dear John.   [*Exit* John.]
—What torments attend a mind in love.   10

AIR LIII, *The Play of Love*

What vast delights must virgins prove,
Who taste the dear excess of love!
    Since while so many ways undone,
    And all our joys must fly from one,
    Eager to love's embrace we run.   15

So when in some small island lies
The eager merchant's brilliant prize,
    That dear, that darling spot to gain,
    He views black tempests with disdain,
    And all the dangers of the main.   20

9. S.D. *Exit* John] *not in GGSO*,
GSO.

8. *spiritual court*] "A court having jurisdiction in matters of religion or ecclesiastical affairs" (*OED*).

[III.ix]   Owen *and* Sweetissa.

OWEN [*aside*].

Sweetissa in tears! So looks the lily after a shower, while
drops of rain run gently down its silken leaves, and gather
sweetness as they pass.—[*To* Sweetissa.]

AIR LIV, *Si Cari*

Smile, smile, Sweetissa, smile;
    Repining banish,   5
    Let sorrow vanish,
Grief does the complexion spoil.
Smile, smile, Sweetissa, smile,
Lift up your charming, cha—a—arming,
    Charming, charming eyes,   10
As the sun's brightest rays in summer skies.

What is the matter, my dear Sweetissa?

SWEETISSA.

Whatever be the matter, it is no matter of yours, Master
Owen.

OWEN.

I would hug thee in my arms and comfort thee, if thou   15
wouldst let me. Give me a buss. Do.

                  [*Attempts to embrace her, but she evades him.*]

AIR LV, *Sleepy Body*

SWEETISSA.   Little master,
                Pretty master,
         Your pursuit give over;
            Surely nature   20
            Such a creature
        Never meant for a lover.
          A beau, and baboon,
          In a dull afternoon,

1. S.D. *aside*] *not in GGSO, GSO.*   16.1. *Attempts . . . him.*] *not in GGSO,*
3. S.D. *To* Sweetissa] *not in GGSO,*   *GSO.*
GSO.

My ladies divert by their capers;   25
    But weak is her head
    Who takes to her bed
    Such a remedy for the vapors.
    Little master, etc.   [*Exit.*]

[III.x]   Owen, *solus.*

AIR LVI

Go, and like a slubb'ring Bess howl,
    Whilst at you griefs I'm quaffing,
For the more you cry, the less you'll—Tol, lol, de rol.
    Be inclined to laughing.

[III.xi]   Owen *and* Susan.

OWEN.

So, Mrs. Susan, which way are you going?

SUSAN.

Going! Why, I am going to find Madam out. If she will
have no victuals, she shall have no cook for Susan. If I cut
the sirloin of beef, may the devil cut me.

AIR LVII, *South-Sea Tune*

An Irishman loves potatoes;   5
A Frenchman chews
    Salads and ragouts;
A Dutchman, waterzuche;
    The Italian, macaroons;
The Scotchman loves sheepsheads, sir;   10

---

29. S.D. *Exit*] *not in GGSO, GSO.*

0.2. *Air LVI*] In the *Genuine Grub-Street Opera* this song is printed as part
of the previous air. If the *Grub-Street Opera* printing represents only a scene
correction, the song should be fitted to the first part of the "Sleepy Body"
air; if, however, it represents a musical correction as well, then the correct
tune has been lost.
[III.xi]
   8. *waterzuche*] i.e., watersouchy. "Fish (properly perch) boiled and served
in its own liquor" (*OED*). Fielding's use is the first recorded in English.
   9. *macaroons*] perhaps macaroons, but more likely macaroni.
   10. *sheepsheads*] "A Virginian Fish of which Broth may be made like
that of Mutton" (Bailey).

> The Welsh with cheese are fed, sir;
> An Englishman's chief
> Delight is roast beef;
> And if I divide the ox' sirloin,
> May the devil cut off mine.   15

OWEN.

Oh, do not spoil thy pretty face with passion. Give me a
kiss, my dear pretty little cook.   [*Attempts to kiss her.*]

SUSAN.

Give you a kiss! Give you a slap in the face, or a rod for your
backside. When I am kissed, it shall be by another guise
sort of a spark than you. 'Sbud! Your head looks like the   20
scrag end of a neck of mutton, just floured for basting. A
kiss! A fart!   [*Exit.*]

[III.xii]   Owen *and* Margery.

OWEN.

Go thy ways, greasy face.—Oh, here's my little Margery
now.

MARGERY.

Not so little neither, Master Owen. I am big enough for you
still.

OWEN.

And so thou art, my dear, and my dove. Come, let us—   5
Let us— Let us—

MARGERY.

Let us what?

OWEN.

Let us, I'gad, I don't know what. Let us kiss like anything.
                    [*Moves toward her. She stops him.*]

MARGERY.

Not so fast, Squire. Your mamma must give you a larger

17. S.D. *Attempts . . . her.*] *not in*   [III.xii]
GGSO, GSO.   8.1. *Moves . . . him.*] *not in GGSO,*
22. S.D. *Exit*] *not in GGSO, GSO.*   *GSO.*
                                          9. must] *GGSO;* just] *GSO.*

9–10. *larger allowance*] Upon coming to England, Prince Frederick had
been allowed £24,000 per year by his father. With other income, his
yearly allowance was £34,000, as contrasted with the £100,000 George II
had been allowed when Prince of Wales. This discrepancy was a constant
bone of contention between Frederick and his parents.

allowance before it comes to that between you and me. 10
Lookye, sir, when you can produce that fine apron you
promised me, I don't know what my gratitude may bring
me to. But I am resolved, if ever I do play the fool, I'll have
something to show for it besides a great belly. *[Exit.]*

OWEN.

Pox on 'em all! I shall not compass one out of the whole 15
family. I'gad I'll e'en go back to Molly, and make sure of
her, if possible. Or I may be in danger of dying half a maid
yet; for the devil take me if I han't a shrewd suspicion that,
in all my amour, I never yet thoroughly knew what a
woman was. I fancy it often happens so among us fine 20
gentlemen.

AIR LVIII

The idle beau of pleasure
Oft boasts a false amour,
As breaking cit his treasure,
Most gaudy, when most poor; 25
But the rich miser hides the stores he does amass,
And the true lover still conceals his happy lass. *[Exit.]*

[III.xiii]   Puzzletext, Robin, *and* John.

PUZZLETEXT.

I will have satisfaction. Speak not to me, Master John, of
anything but satisfaction. I will box him. I will show him
that I was not bred at Oxford for nothing. Splutter! I will
show him my head is good for something else besides
preaching.   *Butts at him.* 5

ROBIN.

You would have armed my head better for butting, I thank
you.

PUZZLETEXT.

You are a lying rascal, and a liar in your teeth.

ROBIN.

You are a liar in your tongue, Doctor, and that's worse.

14. S.D. *Exit*] *not in GGSO, GSO.*   27. *Exit*] *not in GGSO, GSO.*
22. of] *GGSO;* if *GSO.*

21.1. *Air LVIII*] tune unknown.

PUZZLETEXT.

The lie to me, sirrah! I will cut your brains out, if you have   10
any brains. Let me go, John. Let me go—

[*John restrains him.*]

ROBIN.

Let him come; I warrant he goes back again faster than he
came.

PUZZLETEXT.

'Sbud! 'Sbud! 'Sbud!

JOHN.

Fie, Doctor! Be not in such a passion; consider who you are.   15
You must forgive.

PUZZLETEXT.

I will not forgive. Forgiveness is sometimes a sin, ay, and a
damned sin. No, I will not forgive him. —Sirrah, I will
make such an example of you, as shall deter all such
vagabonds for the future, how they affront the church.   20

AIR LIX, *Buff Coat*

In spiritual court,
I'll show you such sport,
Shall make you your own folly curse, sir;
ROBIN.   But you shall be bit,
For I'll stand in the sheet   25
And keep you from handling my purse, sir.

PUZZLETEXT.   In this you'll be shamed,
In the other world damned,
Here a priest, there a devil you'll find, sir;
ROBIN.   I shall know then if priest   30
Or devil be best
At the art of tormenting mankind, sir.

PUZZLETEXT.

Let me go, John. I will— Splutter!—

11.1. John *restrains him.*] *not in*
GGSO, GSO.

[III.xiv]

Sir Owen Apshinken, Lady Apshinken, Puzzletext, Robin, William, John, Susan, Sweetissa, Margery.

LADY APSHINKEN.

Heyday! What's the meaning of this? Mr. Puzzletext, you are not mad, I hope?

PUZZLETEXT.

Splutter! My lady, but I am. I have been abused. I have been beaten.

LADY APSHINKEN.

It cannot be by Robin, I am sure; he's peaceably enough   5
inclined.

WILL.

He'll not strike a blow, unless he's forced to it, I warrant him.

PUZZLETEXT.

Yes, it is by Robin; he hath abused me for writing to his mistress, when I have not had a pen in my hand, save for   10
half a sermon, these six months.

WILL.

Sure letters run strangely in his head! He hath quarreled with me once today, and now he hath quarreled with Mr. Puzzletext, for writing to his mistress. He knows his own demerits, and therefore is jealous of every man he sees for a   15
rival.

ROBIN.

I have not so bad an opinion of myself as to be jealous of you, however sensible you may be of your own merits.

LADY APSHINKEN.

Let us have no quarreling here, pray. —(*Aside to* Robin.) I thought you had more sense than to quarrel with the   20
church.

WILL.

Master may keep you, if he pleases—when he knows you are a rogue. But I'll swear to your stealing the two silver spoons.

SWEETISSA.

You have reason to talk, good Mr. William. I'll swear to   25
your having robbed one of the coaches of the curtains, to

make yourself a waistcoat; and your having stole a pair of buckles out of the harness, and sold them to Mr. Owen, to wear them in his shoes.

SUSAN.

If you come to that, madam, who stole a short silk apron   30 from my lady, and a new flannel petticoat, which you have on at this moment.

JOHN.

Not so fast, good Susan saucebox. Who basted away dozens of butter more than she need, that she may sell the grease? Who brings in false bills of fare, and puts the forged articles   35 in her own pocket? Who wants wine and brandy for sauces and sweetmeats, and drinks it herself?

WILL.

And who wants strong beer for his horses, which he drinks himself?

MARGERY.

I think you should forget that, lest you should be put in   40 mind of the same practice with the coach-horses.

SUSAN.

I suppose when you remember that, you don't forget taking a dram from her ladyship's bottle every time you make the bed.

LADY APSHINKEN.

I can excuse you there, Margery, for I keep all my bottles   45 under lock and key.

SUSAN.

But I suppose your ladyship will not excuse her from a false key, the which I will take my oath she hath now in her pocket.

LADY APSHINKEN.

Very fine, indeed.   50

PUZZLETEXT.

Verily, I am concerned to find my sermons have had no better effect on you; I think it is a difficult matter to determine which deserves to be hanged most; and if Robin the butler hath cheated more than other people, I see no other reason for it, but because he hath had more opportunity to   55 cheat.

ROBIN.

Well said, Parson! Once in thy life thou hast spoken truth.

WILL.

We are none of us so bad as Robin, though there's cheating
in his very name. *Robin* is as much as to say *robbing*.

PUZZLETEXT.

That is none of the best puns Master Will.   60

ROBIN.

Well said, Parson, again!

AIR LX, *Ye Madcaps of England*

In this little family plainly we find,
A little epitome of humankind,
Where down from the beggar, up to the great man,
Each gentleman cheats you no more than he can.   65
  Sing tantarara[ra], rogues all, [rogues all,
  Sing tantararara, rogues all.]

For if you will be such a husband of pelf,
To be served by cheats, you must e'en serve yourself;
The world is so crammed brimful of deceit,   70
That if Robin be a name for a cheat,
  Sing tantarara[ra], Bobs all, Bobs all,
  Sing tantarara[ra], Bobs all.

LADY APSHINKEN.

And have I been raking, and rending, and scraping, and
scratching, and sweating, to be plundered by my servants?   75

SIR OWEN.

Why, truly, my dear, if you had any family to provide for,
you would have had some excuse for your saving, to save
fortunes for your younger children. But as we have but one
son to provide for, and he not much worth providing for,

66–67. *rogues all, . . . rogues all.*] *not
in GGSO, GSO.*

---

59. *Robin . . . robbing*] An essay in *The Craftsman* of June 5, 1731, drew
a resemblance between the words "Robin" and "robbing." *The Grub-Street
Opera* was finished before the essay appeared, but was not published
until later; therefore it is now impossible to determine whether Fielding
influenced the essay or the essay influenced Fielding.

e'en let the servants keep what they have stole, and much   80
good may it do them.

LADY APSHINKEN.

This is such notorious extravagance!

OMNES.

Heavens bless your good honor!

AIR LXI, *My Name is Old Hewson*

ROBIN.   I once as your butler did cheat you,
                    For myself I will set up now;   85
                If you come to my house I will treat you
                    With a pig of your own sow.

SWEETISSA.   I once did your ladyship chouse,
                    And rob you of trinkets good store;
                But when I am gone from your house,   90
                    I promise to cheat you no more.

WILL.   Your lining I own, like a blockhead,
                    I stole to my utter reproach,
                But you will be money in pocket,
                    If you sell off your horses and coach.   95

SUSAN.   My rogueries all are confessed,
                    And for a new maid you may look;
                For where there's no meat to be dressed,
                    There is little need of a cook.

CHORUS.   And so we all give you warning,   100
                    And give you a month's wages too,
                We all go off tomorrow morning;
                    And may better servants ensue.

[III.xv]   *To them,* Owen *and* Molly.

OWEN. MOLLY.

Your blessing, sir.

SIR OWEN. LADY APSHINKEN.

How?

---

88. *chouse*] See *GSO* Introduction, l. 54, n.

OWEN. MOLLY.

We are your son and daughter.

SIR OWEN.

My son married to the daughter of a tenant!

OWEN.

Oh sir, she is your tenant's daughter, but worthy of a crown.   5

AIR LXII, *Fond Echo*

MOLLY.   Oh think not the maid whom you scorn,
    With riches delighted can be!
Had I a great princess been born,
    My Owen had dear been to me.
On others your treasures bestow,   10
    Give Owen alone to these arms,
In grandeur and wealth we find woe,
    But in love there is nothing but charms.

OWEN.   In title and wealth what is lost,
    In tenderness oft is repaid;   15
Too much a great fortune may cost,
    Well purchased may be the poor maid.
While fancy's faint dreams cheat the great,
    We pleasure will equally prove;
While they in their palaces hate,   20
    We in our poor cottage may love.

SIR OWEN.

She sings delightfully, that's the truth on't.

OWEN.

T'other song, t'other song. Ply him with songs till he forgives
us.

AIR LXIII, *Lass of Patie's Mill*

MOLLY.   If I too high aspire,   25
    'Tis love that plumes my wings,
Love makes a clown a squire,
    Would make a squire a king.
What maid that Owen spies,
    From love can e'er be free?   30
Love in his laced coat lies,
    And peeps from his toupee.

SIR OWEN.

I can hold out no longer.

LADY APSHINKEN.

Nor I; let me see you embrace one another, and then I'll
embrace you both.   35

AIR LXIV, *Caro Vien*

MOLLY.	With joy my heart's o'erflowing,
OWEN.	With joy my heart's jolly;
MOLLY.	Oh my dearest sweet Owen!
OWEN.	Oh my charming Molly!

Since I am happy myself, I will make others so. —These   40
letters, Robin, which caused all the jealousy between you
and Sweetissa, I wrote out of a frolic.

ROBIN.

Ha! And did I suspect Sweetissa falsely?

SWEETISSA.

And did I suspect my Robin?

ROBIN.

Oh, my Sweetissa, my sweet.   45

SWEETISSA.

Oh, my Robin, my Bob.

ROBIN.

This hour shall make us one. —[*To* Puzzletext.]   Doctor,
lead to church.

WILL.

What say'st thou, Susan; shall we follow our leaders?

SUSAN.

Why faith, I am generally frank you know, and speak my   50
mind. —I say, yes.

JOHN.

And thou, Margery?

MARGERY.

I do not say no.

PUZZLETEXT.

I am ready to do your business whenever you please.

47. S.D. *To* Puzzletext.] *not in*
GGSO, GSO.

OWEN.

> Look ye, as I have married first, I desire my wedding may   55
> be celebrated first, at least with one dance, for which I have
> prepared the fiddles.

PUZZLETEXT.

> And for which I have prepared my fiddle too; for I am
> always *in utrumque paratus.*   [*Gets ready to play a fiddle.*]

OWEN.

> This day shall be a day of hospitality, I am resolved.   60

LADY APSHINKEN.

> And I am resolved not to see it, and would advise you not
> to be extravagant in it.   *A dance here*

AIR LXV, *Little Jack Horner*

PUZZLETEXT.

> Couples united,
> Ever delighted,
> May they ne'er disagree!   65

WOMEN.

> First we will wed,

MEN.

> Then we'll to bed;

OMNES.

> What happy rogues are we!

CHORUS.

> Couples united,
> Ever delighted,   70
> May we ne'er disagree!
> First we will wed,
> Then we'll to bed;
> What happy rogues are we!

                                               [*Exeunt omnes.*]

FINIS

59. S.D. *Gets . . . fiddle.*] *not in GGSO,*   74.1. *Exeunt omnes.*] *not in WO,*
GSO.   *GGSO, GSO.*

---

59. *in utrumque paratus*] in readiness for anything at all.

Appendix A

The Revisions

From 1730 to 1734 Fielding revised five plays that were proving to be box-office attractions. There is little need to deny that his aim was to increase the popularity of the plays; but the revisions also show that he was objective about his work and that he was developing dramaturgic skills. The growth of *The Grub-Street Opera* is a case in point. In *The Welsh Opera* Fielding had a popular but incomplete piece; in *The Grub-Street Opera* he developed his characters and incidents so that the conclusion of the revised play is logical and satisfying. *The Genuine Grub-Street Opera* is anomalous in this development; the text is not reliable, and though it represents an advanced state of Fielding's revision, it is incomplete.

The plot of *The Welsh Opera*, in two acts, is poorly motivated in comparison with that of the more complex *Grub-Street Opera*. To be more precise, the Owen of *The Welsh Opera* is a palely drawn character. He decides to write his letters for "mischief-sake" after overhearing his mother and Puzzletext discuss his romantic affairs. By contrast, in *The Grub-Street Opera* his machinations are prompted more credibly by his desire for Sweetissa. *The Welsh Opera* does no more than hint at Owen's interest in Molly: the long discussions between them in *The Grub-Street Opera* are not present in the earlier version, and thus Molly's importunate songs in II.vii seem gratuitous, since at that point she makes her first entrance after she has already married Owen. Indeed, her father Apshones is not a person in the drama at all; *The Welsh Opera* does not contain either of the conflicts (added in *The Grub-Street Opera*) in which Owen becomes involved as a result of his love affair.

The same limitation can be seen in the depiction of Owen's parents and in the denouement of *The Welsh Opera*. The parts of Sir Owen and his wife are negligible, Sir Owen appearing in only five scenes and Lady Apshinken in four. In *The Welsh Opera* Fielding introduced a witch, Goody Scratch, to tie up all the loose ends. The omniscient

Goody not only explains the difficulties, but demonstrates that the servants (one of whom, Betty, has only one line) are all members of the gentry who may now step into their birthrights, which uniformly consist of considerable wealth. Though this *deus ex machina* is amusing, it makes *The Welsh Opera* unnecessarily whimsical.

Musically, *The Grub-Street Opera* is a great improvement over *The Welsh Opera*. As Fielding rewrote the play he increased the number of songs from thirty-one to sixty-five, of which fifty-nine appear in *The Genuine Grub-Street Opera*. For the most part the additional music is bright and spirited, and the most important new airs were borrowed from Handel, who at the time was the most popular, as well as the best, English composer. Because of the Handelian compositions, it is fair to say that *The Grub-Street Opera* is musically the most satisfactory of all the ballad operas written in the decade following *The Beggar's Opera*.

A detailed comparison of all three versions of *The Grub-Street Opera* would show that there are many substantive differences even in closely corresponding passages. These differences are too extensive to be described in this appendix. Accordingly, I have included only those passages from *The Welsh Opera* and *The Genuine Grub-Street Opera* which Fielding either omitted from, or revised extensively for, *The Grub-Street Opera*. The prefatory material from *The Welsh Opera* is included first.

[Welsh Opera]   THE PREFACE

As the performance of *The Grub-Street Opera* has been prevented by a certain influence which has been very prevailing of late years, we thought it would not be unacceptable to the Town if we communicated to them *The Welsh Opera*, from which the other was not only originally borrowed, but   5
which is in effect the same, excepting some few additions, that were made only with a view to lengthen it.

The public having given a very kind reception to all productions of this nature that have appeared for some time, we have reason to hope that this, which we flatter ourselves   10
is not inferior to them, will likewise meet with their acceptance; we have reason to hope so, I say, because the characters are affecting, as they may be every man's lot who runs his neck into the marriage noose, since everyone who marries

is liable to have a domineering wife, who will aspire at   15
wearing the breeches, though G—d help the men whose
hard lot it is to fall under petticoat government. A Presbyterian lecture is, I believe, no very agreeable amusement to
any man of sense, especially if it is, as most of them are, very
long winded, but it is my opinion that a curtain lecture is   20
ten times more disagreeable as it is generally something
more sonorous, and much more long winded; for set a
woman's clack but once a-going, and the devil himself can't
stop it, till the alarm, like that of a clock, runs down of
itself. We have known in history that even sovereign princes   25
have not been exempted from such female furies; even one
of the most arbitrary emperors of Turkey had a Roxolana
that held his nose to the grindstone. But I will not anticipate
the reader's pleasure by detaining him too long in the
porch, but only wish him as much satisfaction in the perusal   30
as I had myself, and then I am sure he will not grudge the
price he pays for it.

THE INTRODUCTION

Scriblerus *and a* Player.

PLAYER.

Upon my word, Mr. Scriblerus, you write plays (or something like plays) faster than we can act them, or the town
damn them; I hope your opera will take up more time in
running than it hath in writing. But pray, why do you call
it a Welsh one, since there is not a word of Welsh in it?   5

SCRIBLERUS.

Because the scene lies in Wales, as the *Village Opera*, because
the scene lies in a village, or the *Scots Opera*, because the
scene lies in Scotland.

PLAYER.

Do you not think the town will expect Welsh in it from its
title?   10

SCRIBLERUS.

No, sir, the town is too well acquainted with modern
authors to expect anything from a title. A tragedy often
proves a comedy, a comedy a tragedy, and an opera nothing

at all. I have seen a tragedy without any distress, a comedy
without a jest, and opera without music.   15

PLAYER.

I wish, sir, you had kept within the rules of probability in
your plot, if I may call it so.

SCRIBLERUS.

It is the business of a poet to surprise his audience, especially
a writer of operas. The discovery, sir, should be as no one
could understand how it could be brought about, before it is 20
made.

PLAYER.

No, and I defy them to understand yours after it is made.

SCRIBLERUS.

Well, but I have a witch to solve all that. I know some
authors who have made as strange discoveries without any
witch at all.   25

PLAYER.

You have been kind indeed to lay your jealousy with a witch,
and it would have been as kind in you to have brought in a
conjurer to have raised it. For I am mistaken if any but a
conjurer can imagine how it is raised.

SCRIBLERUS.

Jealousy, sir, is an unaccountable passion. One man is   30
jealous from the beauty of his wife, another from her wit, a
third from her folly, and a fourth from his own folly.

PLAYER.

And a fifth from the folly of the poets. But I think jealousy
a tragical passion, and more proper to tragedy than comedy.

SCRIBLERÜS.

Oh fie, you might as well say that smiles are not proper to 35
tragedy. There is your tragical jealousy, and comical
jealousy. Your tragical jealousy is between kings and heroes,
your comical between gentlemen and servants; your tragical
produces its effect before it is discovered; your comical is
discover'd before its effect; and as in tragedy all die, so in 40
comedy all are married.

PLAYER.

And it is a question, which is the most tragical end of the
two.

SCRIBLERUS.

Smiles are also tragical and comical. The [*makes sad face for audience*] so have I seen, belongs to tragedy. The [*makes happy* 45 *face for audience*], as then to comedy. I think, I may say, the smiles I have introduced in this opera are all entirely new, not like anything that has been produced before.

PLAYER.

No, upon my word, they are as unlike anything else as they are the things they are compared to. 50

SCRIBLERUS.

Sir, if a smile be very unlike, it is as well as if it be very like. So have I not seen is as well as so have I seen. And agad, I don't know whether it does not sometimes surprise more.

PLAYER.

Sir, I wish you would be so kind to stay here to comment upon your opera as it goes on. 55

SCRIBLERUS.

Hey, to be a sort of walking notes.

Enter Second Player.

SECOND PLAYER.

Sir, Mr. Davenport will not go on without a pair of white gloves, and Mrs. Jones, who played Huncamunca, insists on a dram before she goes on for Madam Apshinken. As for Mrs. Clark, the king has fall'd so heavy upon her that he 60 has almost squeezed her guts out, and it's a question whether she will be able to sing or no.

SCRIBLERUS.

Pox on 'em! Bid 'em begin anyway. I'll burn my four dozen of operas and six dozen of tragedies, and never give 'em another. [*Exit*] 65

PLAYER [*to* Second Player].

Good gods, what a fury is an incensed author. [*Exeunt.*]

[For *The Grub-Street Opera* Fielding wrote a new introduction, a draft of which was published in *The Genuine Grub-Street Opera*. Since the first four speeches in this draft closely parallel those in the final version of the Introduction (ll. 1–15), the following excerpt begins with the fifth speech. The *Player* of *The Grub-Street Opera* is here represented by the *Master of the Playhouse*.]

MASTER.

No one, I dare swear, disputes the interest of Grub Street. But, methinks, it is pity your society doth not hang nearer together, that you copy wits in their worst part, and pull one another to pieces as you do, especially in your political pamphlets. 20

SCRIBLERUS.

Why those are all of our society, it's true. But alas, you mistake altercation or scolding a little in jest, for quarreling in earnest. Sir, was you ever at Westminster Hall?

MASTER.

Often, sir.

SCRIBLERUS.

Did you never hear our people scold there? 25

MASTER.

I have heard the lawyers.

SCRIBLERUS.

The lawyers! Why those are our people; there hath long been the strictest union between Grub Street and the law. Thus our politicians are as good friends as our lawyers, behind the curtain. They scold and abuse one another in 30 the persons of their masters and clients, and then very friendly get drunk together over their booty. Our people no more quarrel in earnest than they quarrel with civility. Why sir, you might as well suppose Robin and Will, in my opera, to be in earnest. 35

MASTER.

Why faith, they abuse one another so heartily that I scarce knew at the rehearsal whether they were in earnest or in jest.

SCRIBLERUS.

Ay, have I not wrought up that altercation scene to the height? Let Grub Street alone for that. With what spirit do Robin and Will rap out the lie at one another for half a page 40 together? And let me tell you, sir, the whole wit of Grub Street lies in these two words—you lie.

MASTER.

Which sufficiently proves the whole state of politics to lie in Grub Street.

SCRIBLERUS.

Ay, ay, sir, everything lies in Grub Street. 45

MASTER.

I wonder, considering your interest, you do not obtain some
privileges for your society.

SCRIBLERUS.

It will not be, sir, it will not be. Grub Street, like virtue,
must reward itself; for, whatever interest we have in other
societies, we have none in the Parliament House.   50

MASTER.

But I believe, sir, it is now time to see what interest you have
in this house.

SCRIBLERUS.

With all my heart. I will speak half a dozen of lines to the
audience, and wait upon you, immediately.

Our author does, in humble scenes, produce . . .   55

[The Introduction concludes with the same lines as the Introduction
to *The Grub-Street Opera*, ll. 50 ff.

The first act of *The Grub-Street Opera* is virtually the same in all
three versions, the only major change occurring in I.vii, in the
dialogue between Margery and Sweetissa. The following passage is
from *The Genuine Grub-Street Opera*, and corresponds to *The Grub-Street
Opera*, I.vii. 3–19. The parallel passage in *The Welsh Opera* contains
only minor variants.]

MARGERY.

I would not have you build too much on the promises which
men make beforehand; for a certain old author says, men
are frail.

SWEETISSA.

Very true; but as the poet says, there is a difference in men.

MARGERY.

Still another poet says, there are nine bad ones to one good   5
one.

SWEETISSA.

Granting even that, why may not mine be that tithe-sheep?
In a lottery, where there are nine blanks to a prize, everyone
expects that prize for their own ticket.

MARGERY.

Love is indeed like a lottery, because it draws us into an   10
almost certain loss by the allurement of uncertain gain.

—But then it is not like a lottery, because in everything else it is very unlike one.

SWEETISSA.

I take love to be like a mess of pease porridge, where, though there are some bad peas, there are more good ones. 15 But then it is unlike a mess of pease porridge, because there is a difference between a man and pea; you may know a pea by its outside, you can't a man.

MARGERY.

Love is like an olio.

SWEETISSA.

Rather like a dish of soup-meagre. 20

MARGERY.

Not very unlike potatoes.

SWEETISSA.

Because people live mostly upon them in a cottage.

SWEETISSA.

In short, it's like everything.

MARGERY.

And like nothing at all.

[The second act of *The Grub-Street Opera* and *The Genuine Grub-Street Opera* contains major departures from *The Welsh Opera*. There are, however, the following similarities: *WO* II.i corresponds to the first part of *GGSO* II.iii and to all of *GSO* II.iii; *WO* II.ii corresponds to a portion of *GGSO* II.iii and to all of *GSO* II.iv; *WO* II.iii corresponds to a portion of *GGSO* II.iii and to all of *GSO* II.vi. The principal difference between *GSO* II and *GGSO* II is that II.i and II.viii of *GSO* are not contained in *GGSO*.

The following scenes from *The Welsh Opera* (II.iv and II.v) are omitted in *The Genuine Grub-Street Opera* and *The Grub-Street Opera*. The music for Airs XXVI and XXVII (misnumbered XXVI in *The Welsh Opera*) is included in Appendix B.]

A Noise of Halloo, Halloo—Thunder and Lightning.

[II.iv]   *To them* Goody Scratch.

GOODY SCRATCH.

Oh save me, save me, save me.

JOHN.

Save you? From what?

GOODY SCRATCH.

Oh from the greyhound, from the greyhounds! They take me
for a hare, and will devour me.

JOHN.

If they take you for a witch, I believe they take you right.   5

THOMAS.

Look if she be quite changed out of the hare's form yet.
She has got the ears, and the scent still.

JOHN.

The greyhounds are gone down on the other side of the
hedge. —Goody Scratch, you have been taken for a witch
a long time, and now I think you are sufficiently proved one.   10

GOODY SCRATCH.

Oh spare my life, and do not take me before the justice; and
I will make your fortunes.

THOMAS.

You shall be hanged, you jade.

[II.v]   *To them* Puzzletext (*out of breath*).

PUZZLETEXT.

Did you see the hare?

THOMAS.

We have gotten the hare safe enough. This is the hare.

GOODY SCRATCH.

Oh spare my life, and I'll confess it all. I am a witch indeed.
I am. And I was the hare that you coursed.

THOMAS.

See, Master. Here are her ears and her scut which I caught   5
hold of before she had changed herself from a hare to a
woman again.

PUZZLETEXT.

Oh Goody Scratch, Goody Scratch. I am sorry to find my
sermons have no better effect; but the true reason is,
because you have seldom come to hear them.   10

AIR XXVI, *A Soldier and a Sailor*

In vain the parson preaches,
Of devils, ghosts, and witches.

> While by each unbeliever,
> He's thought a mere deceiver,
>> Or trifler at the best.   15
> But sure the man who spies, sir,
> A witch with both his eyes, sir,
> With ears and scut of hare, sir,
> And looks enough to scare, sir,
>> Must think a witch no jest.   20

Though to say the truth, I never believed one word of witches myself till this moment.

SUSAN.

I see the reason now that my pot would not boil sometimes, though I blowed my eyes out.

PUZZLETEXT.

Oh Goody Scratch, how sorry am I that any of my flock   25
should come to be hanged.

GOODY SCRATCH.

For God's sake, dear sir, do take pity on me.

PUZZLETEXT.

I will do all I can for thee. I will give thee spiritual advice.
And when thou art hanged, I will for so low a price as ten
groats preach thy funeral sermon—wherein I will say of thee   30
as many good things as if thou hadst died a martyr.

GOODY SCRATCH.

Alack, alack. What comfort will your preaching be to me
when I shall not be able to hear it? But if you will be secret,
and preach nothing of this my misfortune, I will discover a
secret that shall make you all rich and happy.   35

OMNES.

Ay, let's hear that.

GOODY SCRATCH.

In the first place you are all people of quality and great
fortunes. You ladies are all daughters of my Lord Truelove.
And you gentlemen are all sons of Sir George Wealthy.

OMNES.

How?   40

GOODY SCRATCH.

On your right arms, ladies, you will find a star, which was
the particular mark of Lord Truelove's children.

OMNES.

How?

PUZZLETEXT.

A star; that was indeed the mark by which they all were known. I do remember to have myself seen that mark when   45
I christened 'em, as being at that time chaplain to my lord.

OMNES.

How?

GOODY SCRATCH.

You, gentlemen, will find behind every one of your ears a swelling, which has been reputed to have been the symptom of an unhappy death, but was indeed no other than a mark   50
placed there by Nature to be the witness of a happy birth.

OMNES.

How?

PUZZLETEXT.

I do remember likewise to have heard a brother clergyman, who was at that time chaplain to Sir George, to have spoken hereof.   55

WOMEN [*showing their arms*].

We have all the marks upon our arms.

MEN [*showing their ears*].

And we behind our ears.

GOODY SCRATCH.

How you came here, I shall tell some other time. Let it suffice now that you ladies are worth nineteen thousand three hundred and fifty-five pounds apiece. —And you,   60
Mr. Robin, have an estate of three thousand a year left you by your father. —You, Mr. John, have the same from an uncle. —You, Mr. Thomas, from another uncle. —And you, Mr. William, from a third uncle.

OMNES.

How?   65

GOODY SCRATCH.

There remains one thing to be set to rights, which is concerning those letters, both which were written in my master's frolic in order to occasion a quarrel betwixt you.

OMNES.

How?

GOODY SCRATCH.

What I have said is true, as I'm a witch.   70

ROBIN.

Oh, Sweetissa, can you pardon me?

SWEETISSA.

Heaven knows how willingly.

WILL.

Susan, what say you? Shall you and I make a second couple?

SUSAN.

We follow our leaders, Mr. William.   75

THOMAS.

What say'st thou, Margery?

MARGERY.

I say, yes.

JOHN.

And you, Mrs. Betty?

BETTY.

I don't say no.

PUZZLETEXT.

Let us then to church, where I will marry you all without   80
farther ceremony.

GOODY SCRATCH.

I have but one word more, which is concerning myself. I
am a widow of five hundred a year jointure, and must
marry a parson to dissolve the spell.

PUZZLETEXT.

Then I have only one word to say for myself, which is, that I   85
may be that parson.

GOODY SCRATCH.

Agreed.

PUZZLETEXT.

I will send for my neighbor Concordance, and he shall
marry us as soon as I have tacked the others together.

AIR XXVII, *Country Bumpkin*

Come to church my lads and lasses,   90
　　First be wedded,
　　Then be bedded,
Thank, if pleased with what there passes,
　　Parson of the parish.
But if you repent your flame,   95

And your marriages,
Prove miscarriages,
'Twill avail you naught to blame
The parson of the parish.

CHORUS.   Who ties the wedding noose,   100
'Tis the parson,
'Tis the parson,
Who's the Hymen for our use,
The parson of the parish.   *[Exeunt omnes.]*

[The concluding three scenes of *The Welsh Opera* correspond to three of the fifteen scenes in Act III of both *The Grub-Street Opera* and *The Genuine Grub-Street Opera*. The following passage from the first of these scenes (*The Welsh Opera*, II.vi) is parallel with *The Grub-Street Opera*, III.ii.5–45.]

MR. AP-SHINKEN.

My wife is a very good wife, but she has an extraordinary tongue of her own. It is happy for me she has servants to scold, for no living man would be able to stand alone the fury of her tongue.

MRS. AP-SHINKEN.

Mr. Ap-Shinken, Mr. Ap-Shinken, it is very well known what offers I have refused when I married you.

MR. AP-SHINKEN.

Yes, my dear. But if you had ever had better, I believe you know your own interest too well to have refused it. Besides, it is a little strange that you should scruple the government of your maids, when you formerly used to dispute with me the government of my men. Thus it is always with women. I will maintain it to be as difficult to please a woman as to shoot a swallow flying. A woman is just opposite to a turnstile, that turns every way with you; she turns every way against. A scolding wife is a kennel of hounds.

MRS. AP-SHINKEN.

A drunken husband is a hogshead of strong beer continually running about the house.

MR. AP-SHINKEN.

A scolding wife is a walking bass viol out of tune.

MRS. AP-SHINKEN.

A drunken husband is a bad fiddlestick, never able to put her into tune or play any tune upon her.

MR. AP-SHINKEN.

A scolding wife is rosin to that fiddlestick, continually rubbing it up to play till it wears it out.

MRS. AP-SHINKEN.

A drunken husband is a wet piece of paper to that rosin, which consumes the rosin without any rubbing at all.

MR. AP-SHINKEN.

The wife is the paper mill that hammers the paper.

MRS. AP-SHINKEN.

And the husband is a paper mill without any hammer at all.

[Act II, Scene vii of *The Welsh Opera* is largely retained in *The Grub-Street Opera*, III.xv (*GGSO* III.xiv), with one major excision and the addition of material concluding the scene. The excision is the following speech by Sir Owen, which in *The Welsh Opera* is printed immediately after the speech corresponding to *The Grub-Street Opera*, III.xv.35.]

MR. AP-SHINKEN.

How little does my lady wife think that this Owen, whom we have bred up as our son, is really the son of our tenant: and this Molly, who is supposed to be the daughter of our tenant, is really our own daughter. But the discovery of this, and of the reasons which induced me to this, I shall defer till some other opportunity.

[In *The Welsh Opera*, "Scene the Last," which follows here, concludes the play immediately after the song by Owen and Molly to the music of Handel's "Caro Vien." This concluding scene corresponds to *The Grub-Street Opera*, III.xv.40 ff.]

SCENE *the Last.*
Omnes.

MRS. AP-SHINKEN [*showing surprise as the married couples enter*].

Hey-day, hey-day! What's the meaning of this?

PUZZLETEXT [*going to her*].

Hearkee, madam.   *Whispers.*

MR. AP-SHINKEN [*as Puzzletext and Mrs. Apshinken confer*].

I suppose my lady will put an end to this diversion immediately.

MRS. AP-SHINKEN [*to* Puzzletext].

How? Men and women of quality?   5

PUZZLETEXT.

As I tell you I assure you.

MRS. AP-SHINKEN.

Then, gentlemen and ladies, I ask your pardon for using you
as servants, not knowing the respect which was due to you.
But I will try to make amends by the hospitality I will show
you this day.   10

OWEN.

If you please we will begin our hospitality with a dance, for
which the fiddles I have provided for my own wedding will
be very opportune.

MRS. AP-SHINKEN.

Be not too extravagant of your hospitality, Owen, neither.

A Dance here.

AIR XXX, *Little Jack Horner*

PUZZLETEXT.   Thus couples united, . . .   15

[The play concludes with this song, as in *The Grub-Street Opera*,
III.xv.63 ff.]

Appendix B

The Music

Without exception, the music that Fielding identified with ballad names is recoverable; that music is included in this appendix. The music for the unidentified airs is lost, probably because it was to have been especially composed by the music director of the New Theatre in the Haymarket. However, for two of these airs (I and LVI) I have ventured to draw upon the earlier versions of the play: the music for Air I is therefore presented as that of "A Lusty Young Smith," and I have suggested that Air LVI could be set to the tune of "Sleepy Body" (see explanatory note to text). For the benefit of any potential directors of a performance of *The Grub-Street Opera*, I suggest that Air XXI could be expediently fitted to the music of "Now Ponder Well": it has always seemed to me that this air clearly recalls the context of Polly's song to her parents in *The Beggar's Opera*, Air 12 (the music may be found in Charles Woods's edition of *The Author's Farce* [Lincoln, Nebr., 1966], p. 136). Also, Air XLVII of *The Grub-Street Opera*, another unidentified tune, might be fitted to the music of Air XLVI, perhaps with burlesque accompaniment. Such a selection would nicely balance the scene in which Airs XLVI and XLVII appear. If these two suggestions were followed, a production of *The Grub-Street Opera* could be mounted with only two tunes lacking (Airs XLI and LVIII).

In determining the music to be selected for this appendix, whenever possible I have taken versions printed in John Watts's editions of Fielding's other ballad operas. When no such version is available, I have first of all preferred John Watts's editions of other ballad operas that Fielding almost certainly saw performed in the theater (e.g., *The Beggar's Opera*, *The Highland Fair*, *The Fashionable Lady*). As the next best sources I have selected versions from ballad operas published as close as possible to 1731. My assumption in both practices has been that the versions selected are likely the ones that Fielding knew and therefore the ones he intended for performance. When no printed plays contain the desired ballad tunes, I have relied on the most authoritative sources I could find (e.g., single-sheet editions in the British Museum and elsewhere, D'Urfey's *Wit and Mirth*, Watts's *Musical Miscellany*). The source for each tune is identified in this appendix, as are the composers, when known.

In fitting the lyrics to the various tunes, I have found that in most instances Fielding's words conform easily to the requirements of the music; there is a natural blend of word and note. The creation of two eighth notes where there is a quarter note in the musical source, and similar minor changes, have marked the extent of my musical alterations. Occasionally, a musical source clearly requires that certain words, phrases, and lines need to be repeated; when this situation has arisen I have made the necessary changes in Fielding's lyrics (e.g., Airs III, XXVII, XLIX, LIV). In all problematical cases, I have tried to find solutions in eighteenth-century sources. Thus, the original words of tunes borrowed by Fielding for *The Grub-Street Opera* sometimes have pointed the way in which Fielding's words may be fitted to the tunes (for example, in arranging the first air, I followed closely Leveridge's original lyrics for "A Lusty Young Smith"; and the form of Handel's "Caro Vien" was the guide for Air LXIV). In all cases, I have studied the arrangements of original words and tunes, and in addition I have also studied other ballad operas in which the tunes used by Fielding appeared. In a number of instances (e.g., Airs XIX, XLVIII), I followed the lyrical fittings made by Mr. Seedo, who was the music director with whom Fielding worked from late 1731 to 1734 (see my "Mr. Seedo's London Career and His Work with Henry Fielding," *Philological Quarterly*, XLV [1966], 179–190). Seedo made the settings for *Songs in the Lottery* (1732) and adapted a few of the lyrics from *The Grub-Street Opera* for *The Lottery*; his fittings have the best claim to authenticity of all. In difficult instances in which there is no eighteenth-century model, I have attempted to make my fittings conform to common sense. For fittings that may seem arbitrary to the musical reader, I assume responsibility.

In songs having more than one stanza, my general principle of arrangement has been to fit only the first stanza to the music, except for Airs I, XLV, and L, which would cause special difficulties if both stanzas were not presented.

AIR I — A Lusty Young Smith — *Richard Leveridge*

What a wretch - ed life Leads a man a ty - rant wife,— While for

each small fault, each small fault he's cor - rec - ted, ho! One

bot - tle makes a sot,— One girl,— One girl,— One girl is

ne'er for - got, And du - ty, and du - ty is al - ways neg - lect - ed,

ho! But though noth-ing can be worse Than this fell do - mes - tic

curse, Some com - fort, com - fort this may do you,

ho! So vast are the hen - pecked bands, That each

neigh-bor, each neigh-bor, each neigh - bor may shake hands, With my

hum - ble, hum - ble ser - vice to you, ho!

AIR II
Lads of Dunce
anon.

If love gets in - to a sol - dier's heart, He puts off his hel-met, his

bow, and his dart. A - chil - les, charmed with a

nymph's fair eye, A dis - taff took, and his

arms laid by. The gay gods of old their

heav - 'n would quit, And leave their am - bro - sia for a

mor - tal tit - bit; The first of that tribe, that

whore-mas-ter Jove, Pre-fered to all heav-'ns, the heav - en of love.

AIR III   Let the Drawer Bring Clean Glasses   *G. F. Handel*

How curst the pu-ny lov-er! How ex-qui-site the pain, When love is fum-bled ov-er, To view the fair's dis-dain! But oh! how vast the bless-ing! But oh! how vast the bless-ing! Whom to her bos-om press-ing, She whis-pers, while car-ess-ing, Oh! when shall we a-gain? Oh! when shall we a-gain? Oh! when shall we a-gain?

AIR IV   March in Scipio   *G. F. Handel*

Think, might-y sir, ere you__ are un-done, Think who__ you are, Ap - shink - en's on - ly son; At Ox-ford you have been, at Lon - don eke al - so; You're al - most half a man, and more than half a beau: Oh do not then dis-grace the great ac - tions of your life! Nor let Ap-shin-ken's son be bur - ied in his wife.

AIR V   Sir Thomas I Cannot   *anon.*

The   worn-out rake   at pleas-ure rails, And cries, 'tis all   i - dle and

fleet - ing;   At   court, the man whose int - 'rest fails,   Cries,

all   is   cor-rup-tion and cheat - ing: But would   you know   Whence

both   these flow? Though so much they pre - tend to   ab - hor them? That

rails   at   court, This at   love's sport, Be - cause they are nei-ther fit

for 'em,   fit for 'em, Be - cause they are nei-ther fit   for 'em.

AIR VI   One Evening Having Lost My Way   *Burkhead* (?)

I've heard a non - con par - son preach 'Gainst whor - ing, with

just dis-dain; Whilst he him - self to be naught did teach Of

fe - males as large a train As stars in the sky, or

lamps in the street, Or beau - ties in the Mall we meet, Or

as, or as, or as, Or as whores in Drur - y Lane.

AIR VII, Part 1   Dutch Skipper   *anon.*

PUZZLETEXT

The gaud-y sun a-dorn - ing With bright-est rays the morn - ing, the

morn - ing, Shines o'er the East - ern hill; And I will go a-sport - ing, And

I will go a-court - ing, a-court - ing, There lies my pleas - ure still.

PUZZLETEXT

In Gaf - fer Wood-ford's ground, A brush-ing hare is found, A

course which e - ven kings them-selves might see; And in a-noth-er place There

lies a brush-ing lass, Which will give one ten times more sport than she.

AIR VII, Part 2   Dutch Skipper   *anon.*

PUZZLETEXT

What pleas - ure to see, while the grey - hounds are run - ning, Poor

puss's cun - ning, and shift-ing, and shun-ning! To see with what art she plays

still her part, And leaves her pur - su - ers a - far: First

this way, then that; First a stretch, and then squat, Till quite out of breath, She

OWEN

yields her to death. What joys with the sports-man's com-pare? How

sweet to be - hold the soft bloom - ing lass, With blush - ing face, clasped

close in em-brace! To feel her breasts rise, see joy fill her eyes, And

glout on her heav'n of charms! While sigh - ing and whin-ing, And

twist - ing   and   twin - ing, With kiss   -   ing and   press   -   ing, And

fond - est   car - ess - ing,   With raptures   she   dies   in   your   arms.

AIR VIII   Bessy Bell and Mary Gray   *anon.*

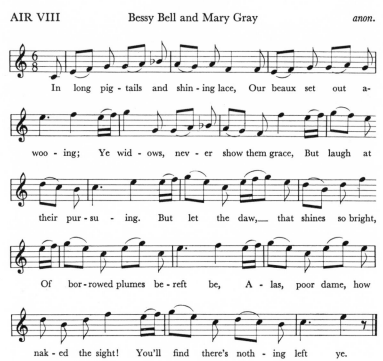

In   long   pig - tails   and   shin - ing lace,   Our   beaux   set   out   a-

woo - ing;   Ye   wid - ows,   nev - er   show them grace,   But   laugh   at

their   pur - su - ing.   But   let   the   daw,__   that   shines   so bright,

Of   bor - rowed plumes   be - reft   be,   A - las,   poor   dame,   how

nak - ed   the sight!   You'll   find   there's   noth - ing   left   ye.

AIR IX Mad Moll *anon.*

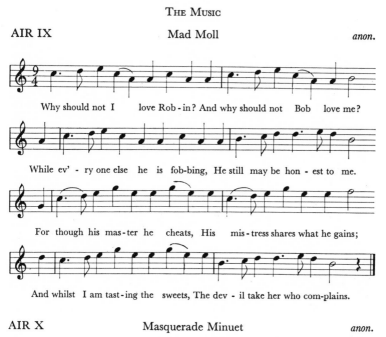

Why should not I love Rob-in? And why should not Bob love me?

While ev' - ry one else he is fob-bing, He still may be hon - est to me.

For though his mas-ter he cheats, His mis-tress shares what he gains;

And whilst I am tast-ing the sweets, The dev - il take her who com-plains.

AIR X Masquerade Minuet *anon.*

ROBIN INSTRUMENT ROBIN

Oh my Sweet-iss - a! Give me a kiss - a,

INSTR. ROBIN INSTR. ROBIN

Oh what a bliss - a To be - hold your

INSTR. ROBIN INSTR.

charms! My eyes with gaz - ing Are set a - blaz - ing.

SWEETISSA

Come then and quench them with-in my arms.

AIR XIII   Ye Nymphs and Sylvan Gods   *John Eccles*

How odd a thing is love, Which the po - ets

fain would prove To be this and that, And the Lord knows what, Like

all things be - low and a-bove. But be - lieve a maid, Skilled e - nough

in the trade Its mys - t'ries to ex - plain; 'Tis a

gen - tle dart, That tick - les the heart, And though it gives us

smart, Does joys im - part, Which large - ly re - quite all the pain.

AIR XIV Red House *anon.*

Ye vir-gins who would mar - ry, Ere you choose, be wa - ___ry,

If you'd not mis - car - ry, Be in - clined to doubt-ing:

Ex - a - mine well your lov - er, His vic-es to dis-cov - er, With

cau - tion con him ov - er, And turn quite in - side

out him; But wed-ding past, The stock - ing cast, The

guests all gone, The cur - tain drawn, Be hence-forth blind, Be

ver - y kind, And find no faults a - bout him.

AIR XV

Black Joke

anon.

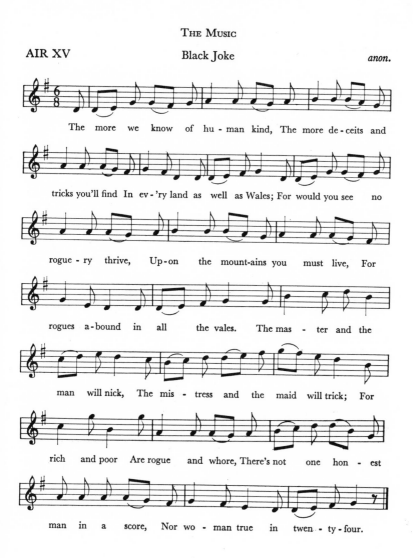

The more we know of hu - man kind, The more de - ceits and
tricks you'll find In ev - 'ry land as well as Wales; For would you see no
rogue - ry thrive, Up - on the mount-ains you must live, For
rogues a - bound in all the vales. The mas - ter and the
man will nick, The mis - tress and the maid will trick; For
rich and poor Are rogue and whore, There's not one hon - est
man in a score, Nor wo - man true in twen - ty - four.

AIR XVI   Tipling John   *Henry Aldrich*

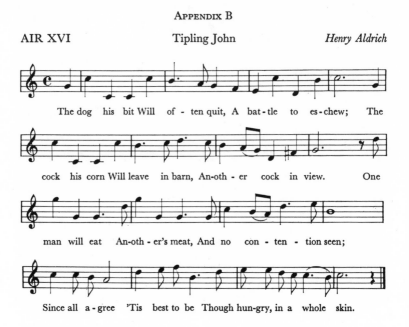

The dog his bit Will of - ten quit, A bat - tle to es - chew; The

cock his corn Will leave in barn, An-oth - er cock in view. One

man will eat An-oth - er's meat, And no con - ten - tion seen;

Since all a - gree 'Tis best to be Though hun-gry, in a whole skin.

AIR XVII   Hedge Lane   *anon.*

In-deed, my dear, With sigh and tear, Your point you will not car - ry;

I'd rath - er eat The of - fal meat, Than oth - ers' leav - ings mar - ry.

Vil - lain, well You would con-ceal Your false - hood by such catch - es; A-

las! too true I've been to you, Thou ver - y wretch of wretch - es.

Well you know What I might do, Would I but with young mas - ter.

Pray be still, Since by our Will, You're now with child of bas - tard.

I with child? Yes, you with child. I with child, you vil - lain? Yes,

you, you, you Mad-am you, you, you Are now with child by Will - iam.

AIR XVIII   Lord Biron's Maggot   *William, Fourth Baron Byron*

Sure naught so dis-as-trous can wom-an be-fall, As to be a good vir-gin, and thought none at all. Had Will-iam but pleased me, It nev-er had teased me To hear a for-sak-en man bawl. But from you this a-buse, For whose sake, and whose use, I have safe corked my maid-en-head up; How must it shock my ear! For what wo-___man can bear To be called a vile drunk-ard, And told of the tank-ard, Be-fore she has swal-lowed a cup?

AIR XIX   Do Not Ask Me   *anon.*

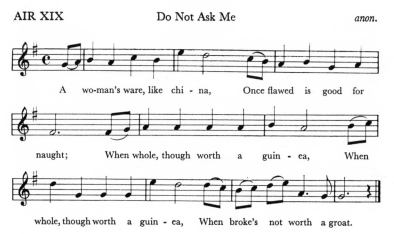

A wo-man's ware, like chi - na,   Once flawed is good for naught;   When whole, though worth a guin - ea,   When whole, though worth a guin - ea,   When broke's not worth a groat.

AIR XX   Tweedside   *anon.*

What wo-man her vir - tue would keep, When naught by her

vir - tue she gains? While she lulls her soft pas - sions a-___

sleep, She's thought but a fool for her pains: Since

val - ets, who learn their lords' wit, Our vir - tue a

bau - ble can call, Why should we our lad - ies' steps

quit, Or have an - y vir - tue at all?

AIR XXII Let Ambition Fire Thy Mind *John Weldon*

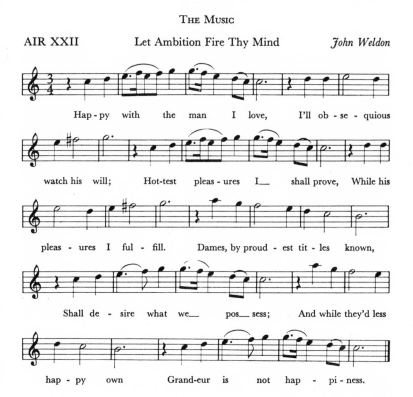

Hap - py with the man I love, I'll ob - se - quious

watch his will; Hot-test pleas - ures I— shall prove, While his

pleas - ures I ful - fill. Dames, by proud - est tit - les known,

Shall de - sire what we— pos— sess; And while they'd less

hap - py own Grand-eur is not hap - pi - ness.

AIR XXIII
Sweet Are the Charms
Richard Leveridge

Beau-ties shall quit their dar - ling town, Lov - ers shall leave the

fra - grant shades, Doc - tors up - on the fee shall frown,

Par - sons shall hate the mas-quer-ades; Nay, ere__ I think of

Ow - en ill, Wo - men shall leave their dear quad - rille.

AIR XXIV
Under the Greenwood Tree
anon.

To wan - ton pleas - ures, rov - ing charms, I bid a long a-

dieu, While wrapped with-in my Mol - ly's arms, I find e - nough in

you. By hous - es this, by hor - ses that, By clothes a third's un - done,

While this a-bides, the sec - ond rides, The third can wear but one.

AIR XXV

Dimi Caro

G. F. Handel

Dear - est char-mer, Dear - est char-mer, Dear-est char - mer, Will

you still bid me tell, What you dis - cern so well By my ex-pir - ing

Fine

sighs, My dot - ing eyes, My dot - ing eyes? Look through th'in-struct-ive

grove, Each ob-ject prompts to love, Hear how the tur - tles coo, Each

D.C. al Fine

ob - ject prompts to love, All na-ture tells you what to do.

AIR XXVI Canny Boatman *anon.*

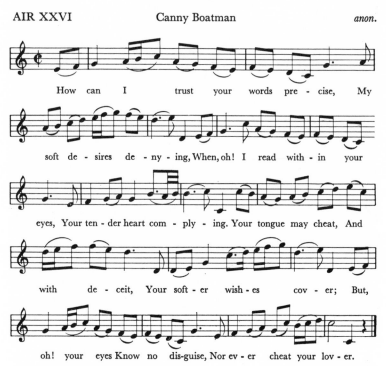

How can I trust your words pre - cise, My

soft de - sires de - ny - ing, When, oh! I read with - in your

eyes, Your ten - der heart com - ply - ing. Your tongue may cheat, And

with de - ceit, Your soft - er wish - es cov - er; But,

oh! your eyes Know no dis-guise, Nor ev - er cheat your lov - er.

AIR XXVII — I'll Range Around — *Henry Carey*

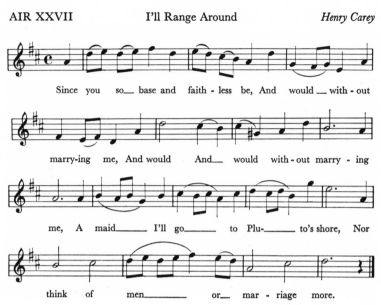

Since you so— base and faith - less be, And would — with - out marry-ing me, And would And— would with - out marry - ing me, A maid_____ I'll go_____ to Plu-_____ to's shore, Nor think of men_____ or— mar - riage more.

AIR XXVIII   Cloe Is False   *G. F. Handel*

Wo-men in vain love's pow'r - ful tor - rent With un-

e - qual strength op-pose; Reas - on a while may

stem the strong cur - rent, Love still at last her soul o'er-

flows; Pleas-ures in - vit - ing, Pas-sions ex - cit - ing, Her lov - er

charms her, Of pride dis - arms her, Down she goes.

AIR XXIX   Britons Strike Home   *Henry Purcell*

Rob-in, come on,   come on,   come on,   As soon as you please.

Will, I will hit thee a slap in the, Slap in the, slap in the face.

Would,   would I could see't,   I   would with both feet, Give thee

such   a kick by the by.   If   you dare, sir, do.   Why

do not, sir,   you? I'm read-y, I'm read-y. And so am I   too.

AIR XXX Mother, Quoth Hodge *anon.*

Oh fie up-on't, Rob-in, Oh fie up-on't, Will. What lang-uage like this, what scul-lion de-fames? 'Twere bet-ter your tongues should ev-er be still, Than al-ways be scold-ing and call-ing vile names. 'Twas he that lies Did first de-vise. The first words were his, and the last shall be mine. You kiss my dog. You're a sly dog. Log-ger-head. Block-head. Fool. Fox. Swine.

AIR XXXI   Dame of Honor   *Thomas D'Urfey*

A wise man oth-ers' faults con-ceals, His own to get more clear of; While fol - ly all she knows re - veals, Sure what she does to hear of. The par - son and the law - yer's blind, Each to his broth-er's err - ing___ For should you search, he knows you'd find No bar - rel the bet - ter her - ring.

AIR XXXII   We've Cheated the Parson   *Henry Purcell*

ROBIN

Here stands hon - est Bob, who ne'er in his life Was known to be guilt - y of fac-tion and strife. But oh what can Ap-pease the man, Who'd rob me of both my place and my wife.

AIR XXXIII   Hark, Hark, the Cock Crows   *Jeremiah Clarke*

When Mas-ter thinks fit,   I'm read-y to quit   A place I so   lit-tle re-

gard, sir;   For while thou art here,   No mer - it must e'er   Ex - pect to find

an - y re - ward, sir.   The groom that is   a - ble To man-age his sta-ble Of

pla - ces   e-nough need not doubt,   sir;   But you, my good broth-er, Will

scarce find an - oth - er,   If   Mas-ter should e'er turn you out,   sir.

AIR XXXIV Of a Noble Race Was Shinken *Thomas D'Urfey*

AIR XXXV Pierot's Tune *anon.*

AIR XXXVI   Country Garden   *anon.*

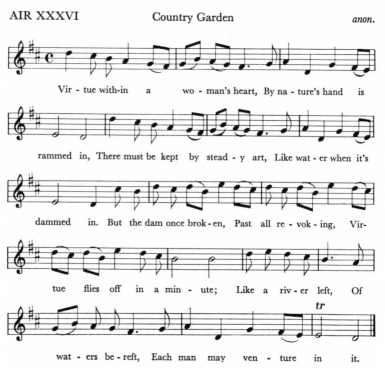

Vir - tue with-in   a   wo - man's heart, By na - ture's hand   is

rammed in, There must be kept by stead - y art, Like wat - er when it's

dammed   in. But the dam once brok - en, Past all re - vok - ing, Vir-

tue   flies off   in a min - ute;   Like a riv - er left,   Of

wat - ers be - reft, Each man may   ven - ture in   it.

AIR XXXVII   Dainty Davy   *anon.*

SUSAN
What   the dev-il mean you thus   Scan-dal scatt'ring, Me be-

spatt'ring, Dir - ty slut, and ug-ly puss, What can be your mean-ing?

SWEETISSA
Had you, mad - am, not for - got, When__ with Bob you__ you know what,

Sure-____ly, mad-am, you would not Twice____ in - quire my mean-ing.

AIR XXXVIII   Valentine's Day   *anon.*

A   wo - man must her hon - or save, While she's   a   vir - gin found;

And he   can hard - ly be   a knave, Who is   not worth a pound.

AIR XXXIX   My Cloe, Why Do You Slight Me   *Lewis Ramondon*

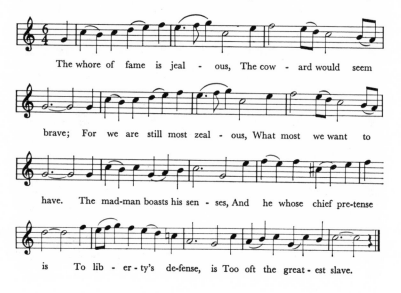

The whore of fame is jeal - ous, The cow - ard would seem

brave; For we are still most zeal - ous, What most we want to

have. The mad-man boasts his sen - ses, And he whose chief pre-tense

is To lib - er - ty's de-fense, is Too oft the great - est slave.

AIR XL Sylvia My Dearest *G. F. Handel*

Cruel - est creat-ure, why have you wooed me, Why thus pur - sued me

In - to love's snare? While I was cru-el, I was your jew - el; Now I am kind,

you bid me des - pair. Na-ture's sweet flow - ers Warm seas - ons nour - ish,

In sum-mer flour - ish, Win-ter's their bane: Love a-gainst na-ture Checked,

grows the great - er, And best is nour - ished with cold dis - dain.

AIR XLII   Midsummer Wish   *Henry Carey*

When love is lodged with - in the heart, Poor vir - tue to

the out-works flies, The tongue in thun - der takes its part, And

darts in light - ning from the eyes. From lips and eyes with

gest - ed grace, In vain she keeps out charm-ing him, For love will

find some weak - er place, To let___ the dear in - vad - er in.

AIR XLIII   Free Mason's Tune   *anon.*

Let the learned talk of books, The glut - ton of cooks, The

lov - er of Cel - ia's soft smack - o; No mor - tal can boast, So

nob - le a toast, As a pipe of ac - cept - ed to - bacc - o.

AIR XLIV　　　　　Tenant of My Own　　　　　*anon.*

Of　all bad sorts of　wives　The scolds are　sure　the　worst,

With　a　hum, drum, scum,　hur - ry scur - ry scum, Would　I'd　a

cuck - old been,　Ere　I　had been ac-cursed With your hum,　drum,

scum,　hur - ry scur - ry scum.　Would　he have cursed man-kind　(If

Ju - no's drawn to　life)　When Jup - i - ter Pan - dor - a sent, He

should have sent　his wife,　With her hum, drum, scum,　hur - ry

scur - ry　scum, With her hum, drum, scum,　hur - ry scur - ry scum.

AIR XLV   The King's Old Courtier   *anon.*

When might - y roast   beef was   the   Eng - lish - man's food,

It en - nob - led our   hearts, and en - rich - ed our   blood,   Our sol - diers

were   brave, and our court-iers were good.   Oh the roast   beef of

Eng - land, And old Eng-land's   roast beef!   But since we have learnt from

all - con - quer - ing France,   To   eat their   ra-gouts as well as to

dance,   Oh what a fine   fig - ure we make in ro-mance!   Oh the

roast   beef of Eng - land,   And old Eng - land's   roast beef!

AIR XLVI Oh Jenny, Oh Jenny *anon.*

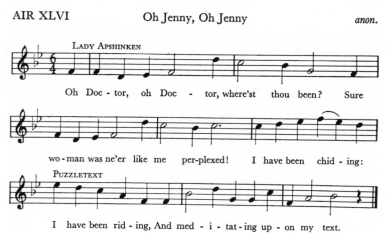

Oh Doc - tor, oh Doc - tor, where'st thou been? Sure

wo - man was ne'er like me per-plexed! I have been chid - ing:

I have been rid - ing, And med - i - tat - ing up - on my text.

AIR XLVIII　　　　　　　In Porus　　　　　　　*G. F. Handel*

Some con-found-ed plan - et　reign-ing,　Sure-ly　hath, be-

yond　ex-plain-ing,　Your sex　　be - guil-ed,　Sense de - fil - ed,

Sense a - wry　led To mis - take:　　I should　won - der,

Could you blun - der　Could you blun - der Thus　a - wake.

But if　　your　al - might - y　wit　　Me for Will - iam

will　　quit,　　E'en brew,　E'en brew As you　bake.

But if　　your al-might-y　wit　　Me for Will-iam will　quit,

E'en　　brew, E'en brew as you bake.　　　Some　con-

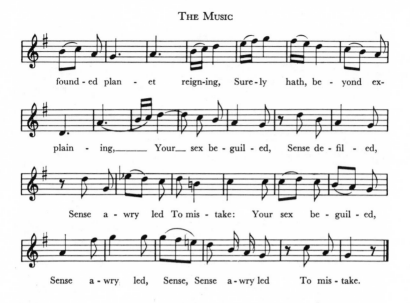

found - ed plan - et reign-ing, Sure-ly hath, be - yond ex-

plain - ing,_____ Your__ sex be - guil - ed, Sense de - fil - ed,

Sense a - wry led To mis - take: Your sex be - guil - ed,

Sense a - wry led, Sense, Sense a - wry led To mis - take.

AIR XLIX   Cupid, God of Pleasing Anguish   *anon.*

What a - vail   large   sums   of   treas - ure,   But to pur - chase

sums   of   pleas - ure,   But your   wish - es   to ob - tain?

Poor the wretch whole worlds pos-sess-ing,   While his dear - est

dar - ling bless - ing   He must sigh for   still   in   vain____

_____.   He must sigh   for

still   in vain.   He__ must sigh   for   still   in   vain.

AIR L   Dame of Honor   *Thomas D'Urfey*

Nice hon - or by   a priv - ate man   With zeal   must   be   main-

tain - ed;   For   soon   'tis lost,   and   nev - er can   By

an - y   be   re - gain - ed.   But once right hon - or - a - ble

grown, He's then   its right - ful own - er;   For though the worst

of   rogues he's known, He   still   is a   man   of hon - or.

AIR LI   Why Will Florella   *Bernard M. Berenclow(?)*

When guilt   with-in____ the bos-_____om lies, A thous-____

and ways it   speaks, It   stares   af - fright - ed   through   the

eyes, And blush-_____ es, And   blush - es through the cheeks. But

in - no - cence, dis - dain-_____ ing fear, A - dorns____

the in - jured face, And while   the   black ac - cus - er's

near, Shines forth,   Shines forth,   Shines forth with bright - er grace.

AIR LII   Hunt the Squirrel   *anon.*

SWEETISSA

Oh for good-ness sake for-bear! Think he's a par - son, think he's a

par - son; Look up - on the cloth he wears, Ere you pull his ears.

ROBIN

Cease your chat-ter-ing, I will bat-ter him; Blood and thund-er - bolt!

I'll rub him, drub him, scrub him down, As jock - eys do a colt.

AIR LIII   The Play of Love   *Pepusch*

What vast de - lights must vir - gins prove, Who taste the dear

ex - cess of love! Since while so man - y ways un-done, And all our

joys must fly from one, Eag - er to love's em-brace we run.

AIR LIV   Si Cari   *G. F. Handel*

Smile,   smile,____ Sweet - iss - a, smile;   Re - pin - ing ban - ish,

Let sor - row, Let   sor - row van - ish,   Grief does   the   com-

plex-_____ion spoil. Smile,   smile____ Sweet - iss - a smile,

Lift up your charm - ing, charm - ing, charm - ing, charm-_____

_____ing eyes,

Lift   up your charm-_____ing eyes,

As____   the sun's bright - est rays_____in sum - mer skies.

AIR LV   Sleepy Body   *anon.*

Lit - tle mas-ter, Pret - ty mas-ter, Your pur - suit give

ov - er; Sure - ly nat-ure Such a creat - ure Nev - er meant for

lov - er. A beau, and bab-oon, In a dull aft - er - noon, My

la - dies div - ert by their cap - ers; But weak is her head Who

takes to her bed Such a rem - e - dy for the vap - ors.

AIR LVII South-Sea-Tune *anon.*

An Ir-ish-man loves po-ta-toes; A French-man chews Sal-ads and

rag-outs; A Dutch-man, wat-er-zu-che; The It-al-ian, mac-a-

roons; The Scotch-man loves sheeps-heads, sir; The Welsh with cheese are

fed, sir; An Eng-lish-man's chief De-light is roast beef; And

if I div-ide the ox' sir-loin, May the dev-il cut off mine.

AIR LIX   Buff Coat   *anon.*

In spir - i - tual court   I'll show you such sport, Shall make you   your

own fol - ly curse, sir.   But you shall be bit,   For I'll stand   in the

sheet,   And keep you from hand - ling my purse, sir.   In this   you'll be

shamed, In   the oth - er world damned, Here a priest, there a   dev - il

you'll find, sir.   I shall know then   if   priest Or   dev - il

be   best   At the   art   of   tor - ment - ing man - kind, sir.

AIR LX   Ye Madcaps of England   *anon.*

In this lit - tle fam - i - ly plain - ly we find   A lit - tle e - pit - o - me of hum - an kind, Where down from the beg - gar, up to the great man, Each gen - tle-man cheats you no more than he can, Sing tan - ta - ra - ra - ra, rogues all, rogues all, Sing tan - ta - ra - ra - ra, rogues all.

AIR LXI   My Name Is Old Hewson   *anon.*

I once as your but-ler did cheat you, For my - self I will set up now; If you come to my house I will treat you With a pig of your own sow.

AIR LXII   Fond Echo   *Gouge(?)*

MOLLY

Oh think not the maid whom you scorn,   With rich - es de-light-ed can

be!   Had I   a great prin-cess been   born,_____ My Ow - en

had dear been to me.   On oth-ers your treas - ures be - stow,

Give Ow - en a-lone   to   these   arms;   In grand - eur and

wealth we find   woe,   But in love there is noth-ing but charms.

AIR LXIII   Lass of Patie's Mill   *anon.*

If I too high a - spire, 'Tis love that plumes my wings,

Love makes a clown a squire, Would make a squire a king.

What maid that Ow - en spies, From love can e'er be free? Love

in his laced coat lies, And peeps from his toup-ee.

AIR LXIV   Caro Vien   *G. F. Handel*

MOLLY

With joy my heart's o'er - flow - ing:

OWEN

With joy my heart's jol-

Oh, my dear - est sweet Ow - en!

ly.   Oh, my charm - ing Mol - ly!

With joy my heart's o'er - flow - ing:

With joy my heart's jol - ly.

Oh, my dear - est sweet Ow - en!

Oh, my charm - ing Mol-

AIR LXV   Little Jack Horner   *anon.*

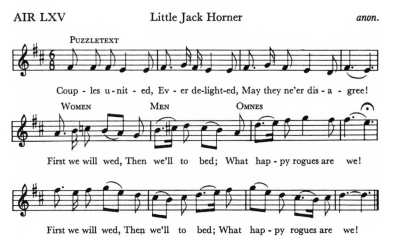

PUZZLETEXT

Coup - les u - nit - ed, Ev - er de-light-ed, May they ne'er dis - a - gree!

WOMEN   MEN   OMNES

First we will wed, Then we'll to bed; What hap - py rogues are we!

First we will wed, Then we'll to bed; What hap - py rogues are we!

THE WELSH OPERA

AIR XXVI　　　A Soldier and a Sailor　　　*John Eccles*

In vain the par - son preach - es, Of dev - ils, ghosts, and witch - es.

While by each un - be - liev - er, He's thought a mere de-

ceiv - er. Or trif - ler at the best, Or

trif - ler at the best. But sure the man who spies, sir, A

witch with both his eyes, sir, With ears and scut of hare,

sir, And looks e - nough to scare, sir, Must think a witch no

jest, Must think a witch no jest.

AIR XXVII Country Bumpkin *anon.*

Come to church my lads and lass - es, First be wedd - ed, Then

be bedd - ed, Thank, if pleased with what there pass - es, Par - son of the

par - ish. But if you re - pent your flame, And your mar - ria - ges,

Prove mis - car - ria - ges, 'Twill a - vail you naught to blame The par - son of the

par - ish. Who ties the wedd - ing noose, 'Tis the par - son, 'Tis the

par - son, Who's the Hy - men for our use, The par - son of the par - ish.

SOURCES

The music for the airs has been taken from the following sources. In all cases, the place of publication for the published works is London. The British Museum has kindly granted permission to reprint the music taken from its Additional Manuscript 29371; this manuscript, which dates from the eighteenth century, is a reliable source of many tunes that were used in the ballad operas, and in a few instances it is the only source.

AIR	I	Brit. Mus. H. 1601 (45).
	II	Add. MS 29371, fol. 30^r (No. 45).
	III	George Lillo, *Silvia* (1731), Air 1.
	IV	John Gay, *Polly* (1729), Air 17.
	V	Henry Fielding, *The Mock Doctor*, 2nd ed. (1732), Air 6.
	VI	John Gay, *The Beggar's Opera*, 1st ed. (1728), Act III, Air 7.
VII, Part 1		John Gay, *Achilles* (1733), Air 10.
VII, Part 2		Seedo, ed.(?), *Songs in the Lottery* (1732), p. 20.
	VIII	Seedo, ed.(?), *Songs in the Mock Doctor* (1732), p. 1.
	IX	Add. MS 29371, fol. 50^r (No. 186).
	X	Anon., *The Jovial Crew* (1731), Air 7.
	XI	Charles Johnson, *The Village Opera* (1729), Air 23.
	XII	*Ibid.*, Air 50.
	XIII	Henry Fielding, *The Virgin Unmask'd*, 1st ed. (1735), Air 15.
	XIV	Add. MS 29371, fol. 49^v (No. 177).
	XV	John Gay, *Achilles* (1733), Air 12.
	XVI	William Chetwood, *The Lover's Opera* (1730), Air 26.
	XVII	*The Dancing Master*, I, 17th ed. (1721), 108.
	XVIII	*Ibid.*, p. 245.
	XIX	Seedo, ed.(?), *Songs in The Mock Doctor* (1732), p. 6.
	XX	Henry Fielding, *Don Quixote in England* (1734), Air 2.
	XXI	Tune unknown.
	XXII	Thomas D'Urfey, ed., *Wit and Mirth*, V (1719), 205.
	XXIII	Charles Johnson, *The Village Opera* (1729), Air 13.
	XXIV	*Ibid.*, Air 44.
	XXV	Henry Fielding, *The Virgin Unmask'd*, 2nd ed. (1735), Air 8.
	XXVI	Joseph Mitchell, *The Highland Fair* (1731), Air 26.
	XXVII	Add. MS 29371, fol. 56^r (No. 222).

XXVIII   Seedo, ed.(?), *Songs in the Lottery* (1732), p. 5.

XXIX   William Chappell, *A Collection of National English Airs* (1840), No. 207.

XXX   Henry Fielding, *Don Quixote in England* (1734), Air 7.

XXXI   Henry Fielding, *The Lottery*, 1st ed. (1732), Air 11.

XXXII   Henry Fielding, *The Virgin Unmask'd*, 1st ed. (1735), Air 14.

XXXIII   Henry Fielding, *The Intriguing Chambermaid* (1734), Air 4.

XXXIV   John Gay, *The Beggar's Opera*, 1st ed. (1728), Act II, Air 13 (G4^v).

XXXV   Henry Fielding, *The Intriguing Chambermaid* (1734), Air 10.

XXXVI   Thomas Walker, *The Quaker's Opera* (1728), Air 20.

XXXVII   Add. MS 29371, fol. 52^r (No. 198).

XXXVIII   Thomas Walker, *The Quaker's Opera* (1728), Air 13.

XXXIX   *The Musical Miscellany*, published by John Watts, II (1729), 113.

XL   *Ibid.*, VI (1731), 74–75.

XLI   Tune Unknown.

XLII   Anon., *Universal Harmony* (1743), p. 75.

XLIII   Seedo, ed.(?), *Songs in the Lottery* (1732), p. 2.

XLIV   William Rufus Chetwood, *The Generous Free-Mason* (1731), Air 19.

XLV   Henry Playford, ed., *Wit and Mirth* (1699), p. 289 [Day and Murrie, *English Song Books, 1651–1702*, No. 182].

XLVI   John Gay, *The Beggar's Opera*, 1st ed. (1728), Act I, Air 9 (G2^r).

XLVII   Tune Unknown.

XLVIII   Seedo, ed.(?), *Songs in the Lottery* (1732), pp. 11 f.

XLIX   *The Musical Miscellany*, published by John Watts, III (1730), 148.

L   Henry Fielding, *The Lottery*, 1st ed. (1732), Air 11 (same as Air XXXI).

LI   Henry Fielding, *Don Quixote in England* (1734), Air 3.

LII   Henry Fielding, *The Lottery*, 1st ed. (1732), Air 15.

LIII   Charles Johnson, *The Village Opera* (1729), Air 8.

LIV   Henry Fielding, *The Lottery*, 1st ed. (1732), Air 18.

LV   James Ralph, *The Fashionable Lady* (1730), Air 28.

LVI   Tune Unknown.

LVII   Seedo, ed.(?), *Songs in the Lottery* (1732), p. 17.
LVIII   Tune Unknown.
LIX   Seedo, ed.(?), *Songs in the Lottery* (1732), pp. 18 f.
LX   *Ibid.*, p. 23.
LXI   Anon., *The Jovial Crew* (1731), Air 19.
LXII   William Rufus Chetwood, *The Generous Free-Mason* (1731), Air 28.
LXIII   Henry Fielding, *The Virgin Unmask'd*, 1st ed. (1735), Air 10.
LXIV   George Frederick Handel, *Porus* (n.d.), p. 79 [Brit. Mus. H. 299. e].
LXV   James Hook, ed., *A Christmas Box* (*c.* 1795–1802), p. 3.

Music for *The Welsh Opera*

AIR XXVI   Thomas D'Urfey, ed., *Wit and Mirth*, III (1719), 220.
XXVII   Ebeneezer Forest, *Momus Turned Fabulist* (1729), Air 40.

Appendix C

Chronology

Approximate dates are indicated by *. Dates for plays are those on which they were first made public, either on stage or in print.

Political and Literary Events	*Life and Major Works of Fielding*
1631	
Death of Donne.	
John Dryden born.	
1633	
Samuel Pepys born.	
1635	
Sir George Etherege born.*	
1640	
Aphra Behn born.*	
1641	
William Wycherley born.*	
1642	
First Civil War began (ended 1646).	
Theaters closed by Parliament.	
Thomas Shadwell born.*	
1648	
Second Civil War.	
Nathaniel Lee born.*	
1649	
Execution of Charles I.	
1650	
Jeremy Collier born.	
1651	
Hobbes' *Leviathan* published.	
1652	
First Dutch War began (ended 1654).	
Thomas Otway born.	

1656
D'Avenant's *THE SIEGE OF RHODES* performed at Rutland House.

1657
John Dennis born.

1658
Death of Oliver Cromwell.
D'Avenant's *THE CRUELTY OF SPANIARDS IN PERU* performed at the Cockpit.

1660
Restoration of Charles II.
Theatrical patents granted to Thomas Killigrew and Sir William D'Avenant, authorizing them to form, respectively, the King's and the Duke of York's Companies.
Pepys began his diary.

1661
Cowley's *THE CUTTER OF COLEMAN STREET*.
D'Avenant's *THE SIEGE OF RHODES* (expanded to two parts).

1662
Charter granted to the Royal Society.

1663
Dryden's *THE WILD GALLANT*.
Tuke's *THE ADVENTURES OF FIVE HOURS*.

1664
Sir John Vanbrugh born.
Dryden's *THE RIVAL LADIES*.
Dryden and Howard's *THE INDIAN QUEEN*.
Etherege's *THE COMICAL REVENGE*.

1665
Second Dutch War began (ended 1667).
Great Plague.

Dryden's *THE INDIAN EM-PEROR*.

Orrery's *MUSTAPHA*.

1666

Fire of London.

Death of James Shirley.

1667

Jonathan Swift born.

Milton's *Paradise Lost* published.

Sprat's *The History of the Royal Society* published.

Dryden's *SECRET LOVE*.

1668

Death of D'Avenant.

Dryden made Poet Laureate.

Dryden's *An Essay of Dramatic Poesy* published.

Shadwell's *THE SULLEN LOVERS*.

1669

Pepys terminated his diary.

Susannah Centlivre born.

1670

William Congreve born.

Dryden's *THE CONQUEST OF GRANADA*, Part I.

1671

Dorset Garden Theatre (Duke's Company) opened.

Colley Cibber born.

Milton's *Paradise Regained* and *Samson Agonistes* published.

Dryden's *THE CONQUEST OF GRANADA*, Part II.

THE REHEARSAL, by the Duke of Buckingham and others.

Wycherley's *LOVE IN A WOOD*.

1672

Third Dutch War began (ended 1674).

oseph Addison born.

Richard Steele born.

Dryden's *MARRIAGE A LA MODE.*

1674

New Drury Lane Theatre (King's Company) opened.
Death of Milton.
Nicholas Rowe born.
Thomas Rymer's *Reflections on Aristotle's Treatise of Poesy* (translation of Rapin) published.

1675

Dryden's *AURENG-ZEBE.*
Wycherley's *THE COUNTRY WIFE.* *

1676

Etherege's *THE MAN OF MODE.*
Otway's *DON CARLOS.*
Shadwell's *THE VIRTUOSO.*
Wycherley's *THE PLAIN DEALER.*

1677

Rymer's *Tragedies of the Last Age Considered* published.
Aphra Behn's *THE ROVER.*
Dryden's *ALL FOR LOVE.*
Lee's *THE RIVAL QUEENS.*

1678

Popish Plot.
George Farquhar born.
Bunyan's *Pilgrim's Progress* (Part I) published.

1679

Exclusion Bill introduced.
Death of Thomas Hobbes.
Death of Roger Boyle, Earl of Orrery.
Charles Johnson born.

1680

Death of Samuel Butler.
Death of John Wilmot, Earl of Rochester.

Dryden's *THE SPANISH FRIAR.*
Lee's *LUCIUS JUNIUS BRUTUS.*
Otway's *THE ORPHAN.*

1681

Charles II dissolved Parliament at
Oxford.
Dryden's *Absalom and Achitophel* pub-
lished.
Tate's adaptation of *KING LEAR.*

1682

The King's and Duke of York's
Companies merged into the United
Company.
Dryden's *The Medal, MacFlecknoe,*
and *Religio Laici* published.
Otway's *VENICE PRESERVED.*

1683

Rye House Plot.
Death of Thomas Killigrew.
Crowne's *CITY POLITIQUES.*

1685

Death of Charles II; accession of
James II.
Revocation of the Edict of Nantes.
The Duke of Monmouth's Rebel-
lion.
Death of Otway.
John Gay born.
Crowne's *SIR COURTLY NICE.*
Dryden's *ALBION AND AL-
BANIUS.*

1687

Death of the Duke of Buckingham.
Dryden's *The Hind and the Panther*
published.
Newton's *Principia* published.

1688

The Revolution.
Alexander Pope born.
Shadwell's *THE SQUIRE OF
ALSATIA.*

1689

The War of the League of Augsburg
began (ended 1697).
Toleration Act.
Death of Aphra Behn.
Shadwell made Poet Laureate.
Dryden's *DON SEBASTIAN*.
Shadwell's *BURY FAIR*.

1690

Battle of the Boyne.
Locke's *Two Treatises of Government*
and *An Essay Concerning Human
Understanding* published.

1691

Death of Etherege.*
Langbaine's *An Account of the English
Dramatic Poets* published.

1692

Death of Lee.
Death of Shadwell.
Tate made Poet Laureate.

1693

George Lillo born.*
Rymer's *A Short View of Tragedy*
published.
Congreve's *THE OLD BACHELOR*.

1694

Death of Queen Mary.
Southerne's *THE FATAL MAR-
RIAGE*.

1695

Group of actors led by Thomas
Betterton left Drury Lane and
established a new company at
Lincoln's Inn Fields.
Congreve's *LOVE FOR LOVE*.
Southerne's *OROONOKO*.

1696

Cibber's *LOVE'S LAST SHIFT*.
Vanbrugh's *THE RELAPSE*.

1697

Treaty of Ryswick ended the War
of the League of Augsburg.

Charles Macklin born.

Congreve's *THE MOURNING BRIDE*.

Vanbrugh's *THE PROVOKED WIFE*.

1698

Collier controversy started with the publication of *A Short View of the Immorality and Profaneness of the English Stage.*

1699

Farquhar's *THE CONSTANT COUPLE*.

1700

Death of Dryden.

Blackmore's *Satire against Wit* published.

Congreve's *THE WAY OF THE WORLD*.

1701

Act of Settlement.

War of the Spanish Succession began (ended 1713).

Death of James II.

Rowe's *TAMERLANE*.

Steele's *THE FUNERAL*.

1702

Death of William III; accession of Anne.

The Daily Courant began publication.

Cibber's *SHE WOULD AND SHE WOULD NOT*.

1703

Death of Samuel Pepys.

Rowe's *THE FAIR PENITENT*.

1704

Capture of Gibraltar; Battle of Blenheim.

Defoe's *The Review* began publication (1704–1713).

Swift's *A Tale of a Tub* and *The Battle of the Books* published.

Cibber's *THE CARELESS HUS-BAND*.

1705

Haymarket Theatre opened.

Steele's *THE TENDER HUS-BAND*.

1706

Battle of Ramillies.

Farquhar's *THE RECRUITING OFFICER*.

1707

Union of Scotland and England.   Born April 22.

Death of Farquhar.

Farquhar's *THE BEAUX' STRA-TAGEM*.

1708

Downes' *Roscius Anglicanus* published.

1709

Samuel Johnson born.

Rowe's edition of Shakespeare published.

The Tatler began publication (1709–1711).

Centlivre's *THE BUSY BODY*.

1711

Shaftesbury's *Characteristics* published.

The Spectator began publication (1711–1712).

Pope's *An Essay on Criticism* published.

1713

Treaty of Utrecht ended the War of the Spanish Succession.

Addison's *CATO*.

1714

Death of Anne; accession of George I.

Steele became Governor of Drury Lane.

John Rich assumed management of Lincoln's Inn Fields.

Centlivre's *THE WONDER: A WOMAN KEEPS A SECRET.*
Rowe's *JANE SHORE.*

1715
Jacobite Rebellion.
Death of Tate.
Rowe made Poet Laureate.
Death of Wycherley.

1716
Addison's *THE DRUMMER.*

1717
David Garrick born.
Cibber's *THE NON-JUROR.*
Gay, Pope, and Arbuthnot's *THREE HOURS AFTER MARRIAGE.*

1718
Death of Rowe.
Centlivre's *A BOLD STROKE FOR A WIFE.*

1719
Death of Addison.
Defoe's *Robinson Crusoe* published.
Young's *BUSIRIS, KING OF EGYPT.*

Entered Eton; remained there until 1725.*

1720
South Sea Bubble.
Samuel Foote born.
Little Theatre in the Haymarket opened.
Steele suspended from the Governorship of Drury Lane (restored 1721).
Steele's *The Theatre* (periodical) published.
Hughes' *THE SIEGE OF DAMASCUS.*

1721
Walpole became first Minister.

1722
Steele's *THE CONSCIOUS LOVERS.*

-159-

1723
Death of Susannah Centlivre.
Death of D'Urfey.

1725
Pope's edition of Shakespeare published.

1726
Death of Jeremy Collier.
Death of Vanbrugh.
Law's *Unlawfulness of Stage Entertainments* published.
Swift's *Gulliver's Travels* published.

1727
Death of George I; accession of George II.
Death of Sir Isaac Newton.
Arthur Murphy born.

1728
Pope's *The Dunciad* (first version) published.
Cibber's *THE PROVOKED HUSBAND* (expansion of Vanbrugh's fragment *A JOURNEY TO LONDON*).
Gay's *THE BEGGAR'S OPERA*.

The Masquerade.
LOVE IN SEVERAL MASQUES (Drury Lane, February 16).
Enrolled at the University of Leyden.

1729
Goodman's Fields Theatre opened.
Death of Congreve.
Death of Steele.
Edmund Burke born.

Returned from Leyden.

1730
Cibber made Poet Laureate.
Oliver Goldsmith born.
Thomson's *The Seasons* published.

THE TEMPLE BEAU (Goodman's Fields, January 26).
THE AUTHOR'S FARCE (Haymarket, March 30).
TOM THUMB (Haymarket, April 24).
RAPE UPON RAPE (Haymarket, June 23).

1731
Death of Defoe.
Lillo's *THE LONDON MERCHANT*.

THE LETTER WRITERS (Haymarket, March 24).
THE TRAGEDY OF TRAGEDIES

[revision of *TOM THUMB*] (Haymarket, March 24).
THE WELSH OPERA (Haymarket, April 22), revised as *THE GRUB-STREET OPERA* (suppressed).

1732
Covent Garden Theatre opened.
Death of Gay.
George Colman the elder born.
Charles Johnson's *CAELIA*.

THE LOTTERY (Drury Lane, January 1).
THE MODERN HUSBAND (Drury Lane, February 14).
THE OLD DEBAUCHEES (Drury Lane, June 1).
THE COVENT GARDEN TRAGEDY (Drury Lane, June 1).
THE MOCK DOCTOR (Drury Lane, June 23).

1733
Pope's *An Essay on Man* (Epistles I–III) published (Epistle IV, 1734).

THE MISER (Drury Lane, February 17).

1734
Death of Dennis.
The Prompter began publication (1734–1736).
Theobald's edition of Shakespeare published.

THE AUTHOR'S FARCE, revised (Drury Lane, January 15).
THE INTRIGUING CHAMBERMAID (Drury Lane, January 15).
DON QUIXOTE IN ENGLAND (Haymarket, April 5).
Married Charlotte Cradock, November 28.

1735
Pope's *Epistle to Dr. Arbuthnot* published.

AN OLD MAN TAUGHT WISDOM (Drury Lane, January 6).
THE UNIVERSAL GALLANT (Drury Lane, February 10).

1736
Lillo's *FATAL CURIOSITY*.

Organized "Great Mogul's Company of Comedians" at the Haymarket.
PASQUIN (Haymarket, March 5).
TUMBLE-DOWN DICK (Haymarket, April 29).

1737

The Stage Licensing Act.
Dodsley's *THE KING AND THE MILLER OF MANSFIELD.*

EURYDICE (Drury Lane, February 19).
THE HISTORICAL REGISTER (Haymarket, March 21).
EURYDICE HISSED (Haymarket, April 13).
Entered the Middle Temple, November 1.

1738

Johnson's *London* published.
Pope's *One Thousand Seven Hundred and Thirty-Eight* published.
Thomson's *AGAMEMNON.*

1739

War with Spain began.
Death of Lillo.
Hugh Kelly born.
Johnson's *Complete Vindication of Licensers of the Stage,* an ironical criticism of the Licensing Act, published after Brooke's *GUSTAVUS VASA* was denied a license.

The Champion began publication (1739–1741).

1740

War of the Austrian Succession began (ended 1748).
James Boswell born.
Cibber's *Apology for His Life* published.
Richardson's *Pamela* published.
Garrick's *LETHE.*
Thomson and Mallet's *ALFRED.*

Called to the bar, June 20.

1741

Edmund Malone born.
Garrick began acting.
Garrick's *THE LYING VALET.*

Shamela published.

1742

Walpole resigned his offices.
Cibber's *Letters to Mr. Pope* published.
Pope's *New Dunciad* (Book IV of *The Dunciad*) published.
Young's *The Complaint, or Night*

Joseph Andrews published.
MISS LUCY IN TOWN (Drury Lane, May 6).

Thoughts published (additional parts published each year until 1745).

1743

Death of Henry Carey.
Pope's *The Dunciad* (final version) published.

Miscellanies published.
THE WEDDING DAY (Drury Lane, February 17).
Death of his wife.*

1744

Death of Pope.
Death of Theobald.
Dodsley's *A Select Collection of Old Plays* published.
Johnson's *Life of Mr. Richard Savage* published.

1745

Jacobite Rebellion.
Death of Swift.
Thomas Holcroft born.
Johnson's *Observations on Macbeth* published.
Thomson's *TANCRED AND SIGISMUNDA.*

1746

Death of Southerne.
Collins's *Odes* published.

1747

Garrick entered the management of Drury Lane Theatre.
Johnson's *Prologue Spoken by Mr. Garrick at the Opening of the Theatre in Drury Lane, 1747.*
Warburton's edition of Shakespeare published.
Garrick's *MISS IN HER TEENS.*
Hoadly's *THE SUSPICIOUS HUSBAND.*

Married Mary Daniel, November 27.

1748

Treaty of Aix-la-Chapelle ended the War of the Austrian Succession.
Death of Thomson.
Hume's *Philosophical Essays Concerning Human Understanding* published.

Appointed Justice of Peace for Westminster.

Richardson's *Clarissa* published.

Smollett's *Roderick Random* published.

1749

Death of Ambrose Philips.

Bolingbroke's *Idea of a Patriot King* published.

Chetwood's *A General History of the Stage* published.

Johnson's *The Vanity of Human Wishes* published.

Hill's *MEROPE* (adaptation of Voltaire).

Johnson's *IRENE*.

1750

Death of Aaron Hill.

Johnson's *The Rambler* began publication (1750–1752).

1751

Death of Bolingbroke.

Richard Brinsley Sheridan born.

Gray's *An Elegy Wrote in a Country Churchyard* published.

Smollett's *Peregrine Pickle* published.

1752

Mason's *ELFRIDA* published.

1753

Death of Bishop Berkeley.

Elizabeth Inchbald born.

Foote's *THE ENGLISHMAN IN PARIS*.

Glover's *BOADICEA*.

Moore's *THE GAMESTER*.

Young's *THE BROTHERS*.

1754

Richardson's *Sir Charles Grandison* published.

Whitehead's *CREUSA, QUEEN OF ATHENS*.

Tom Jones published.

Amelia published.

The Covent Garden Journal published.

Died in Lisbon, October 8.

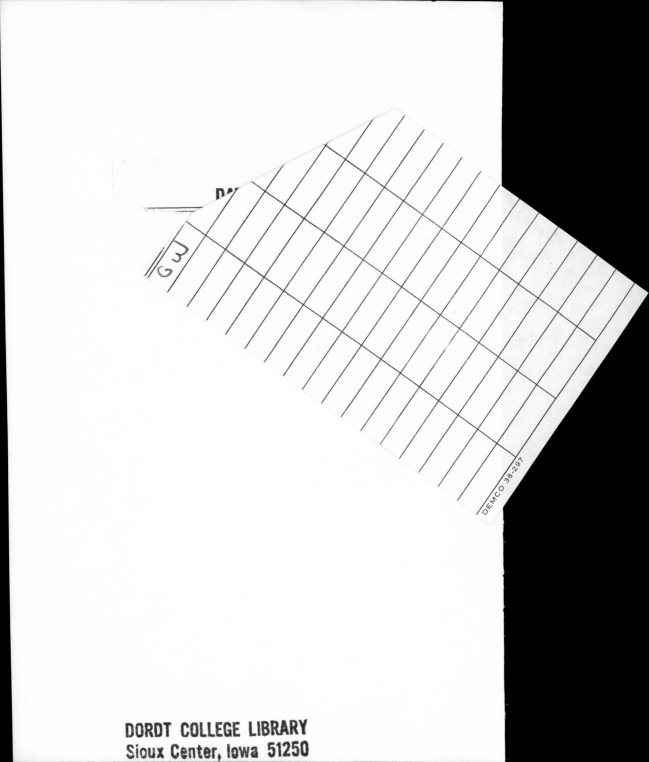